LET ME PERISH FROM STARVATION'S LOVE

by

Limelight

RoseDog Books
PITTSBURGH, PENNSYLVANIA 15238

RoseDog Books
585 Alpha Drive, Suite 103
Pittsburgh, PA 15238
Visit our website at *www.rosedogbookstore.com*

ISBN: 978-1-64957-944-7
eISBN: 978-1-64957-965-2

Mark,

Here is the transcript from my interview with Jay Leno on *The Tonight Show*.

JL: Hi, Miss Nancy. Please tell me about the Princess Project and your experience with Verify.

NS: Okay. It's been a roller coaster of a ride.

JL: How so?

NS: Even before the job was completed, Mark sent out a dissatisfaction survey. He said he only sends these out to customers every ten years.

JL: What kinds of questions did he ask, and what were your responses?

NS: Well, let me think. Was the work completed by the date promised? No completion date was given, although in passing he did mention by the year 2525. Did the workers exhibit a professional attitude? Not sure, although they reminded me of the Three Stooges. Are you satisfied with the quality of workmanship? As long as it keeps the bugs out of my bathroom, it's all good. Was Major Mark in communication with you frequently throughout the process? No, there were spurts when I thought he filed for divorce from me but neglected to inform me of this action. Funny, he did mention that he majored in communications at the College of Abbott and Costello, but I question that statement. Did Loopy Louis finish painting your bathroom? He tried but ran out of paint. He said he would be back but never returned. That reminds me of the story of the guy who tells his wife that he is only going to the store to pick up a pack of cigarettes and never returns. What was your opinion of the master plumber? Well, when you try to save money, you end up with leaks. Lesson learned is pay more, no leaks. On a scale of zero to ten, how happy were you with the work? I'm still waiting for the roofer to fix the leak, and the Keystone Cops to finish the bathroom. Is it true that Major Mark obtained a PhD in engineering? Yes, he indicated to me that he specifically got this so he could put the futon frame together correctly, but unfortunately, his education was sorely lacking. If I were him, I would request a full refund of my tuition. What is Wilberforce? It has something to do with *Star Wars*, and may the force be with you. Would you use his company again in the future? Absolutely. I get my best comedy material from these clowns.

JL: Thanks for agreeing to appear on my show. Have you been booked to appear on other shows?

NS: You bet. Dr. Phil has agreed to give me one-on-one therapy sessions gratis after hearing about my saga. Oprah said she will consider making it a movie of the week; Hallmark said they are considering printing sympathy cards based on my experience; and Ellen has promised me a free igloo in Alaska.

Oct 31, 2014
I know ur days r full with so much work 2 do please be aware my expiration is near pls take pity on me & then we can see when 2 start this project & live happily. I hope u like this poem 4 u it was composed.

Nov 12, 2014
A flush of the toilet & raindrops keep failing on my head in the kitchen. Weird.

Nov 14, 2014
My toilet does not flush but please don't rush perhaps the smell will make the critter flee & then I will be completely squirrel free.

Nov 17, 2014
Good morning. Not 2 be a nag but my monument 2 poop has yielded enough fertilizer 4 my new garden. Have a pain free day.

Nov 18, 2014
Good morning. Thx 4 the new throne. U have VERIFIED that I am truly royalty…

Nov 21, 2014
Please be careful not to disturb floor tile.

Nov 22, 2014
I did not wake the tiles. Have a dry day.

Nov 24, 2014
Tune in 4 the next exciting episode of All My Leaks. We find Princess in the kitchen checking out the drips from under the sink. Raging floodwater outside

her home threaten 2 make her house an ark, sans the animals. Will Leaks McGee fix the problem, or will he masterfully sabotage her faucets? Is Mark able 2 rescue her from the encroaching mold? Don't miss this cliffhanger. We promise it's more suspenseful than who shot JR.

Nov 26, 2014

Preview an upcoming episode of AML. Will Princess flee the tundra of Ohio 4 the warmth of Alaska? As she wonders why her toes are tingling & her fingers have turned 2 stone, Major Mark barks you're in the army now, go take a cold shower Princess. Hot water is reserved 4 the Captain. Meanwhile her almost finished bathroom fixtures & pet squirrel, Sasha, are enjoying the sauna. Will Jolly Jeris grow musical shaped vegetables so Lovely Louis can play & then eat his veggies? Will Renegade Rick be able 2 wire all of Greater Dayton? Stay tuned 4 the shocking conclusion.

Dec 1, 2014

The saga continues. Is Major Mark mean 4 allowing Lefty Louis (name changed approved by LL), aka 1 of the 3 stooges, 2 create a patchwork paint-by-numbers bathroom motif & why is Sasha a magnificent shade of mauve? Will the fashion police arrest LL? Only the shadow knows 4 sure. Will Princess don her I survived the blackout of 2014 tee shirt 4 the next Contractors of America Campaign? Are the remnants of roaches covering her walls a hint 2 create a bug mural? Who is Jazzy Jason? After this operation, will MM be the next disco king, the John Travolta of 5 Oaks? As the plaster continues 2 gently fall, adding color 2 her already white hair, she is reminded of the saying if life hands you plaster, make chalk. According to an analysis by Freud, the reason behind Leaks McGee trails of water stems from his mommy leaving him 2 long in a wet diaper as a tender tot. Thus began Perry Mason's greatest Case of the Drippy Drawers. Why didn't LM show up 2 interview a candidate 4 the secretarial position, was it because he was waiting 4 the bagels 2 be flown in & had 2 personally pick them up at the airport or did he secretly MARRY HIMSELF? Does he suffer from water on the brain? Was the real reason LM left Princess with a cascade of gentle drops so she can wash her dirty floors? And so my friends, we wrap up another season of *All My Leaks*.

Hands

I remember the first time I saw you. Grade school, you recall. Our teacher, Miss Beasley, had us hold hands when we were very small. The next time I noticed your hands, high school we were in. You held the door for me, darling. Bam! I was your best friend. Later on, at our wedding, your strong hands enveloped mine as you promised to care for me always, and then I sighed. Your calloused hands held our newborn and diaper changes you made. They brushed the tears from my pain and mourning. You cradled my heart in those very same strong hands. And when you loved me, you were gentle. You tickled our son and played ball with him every weekend. You built our house and fixed our problems. They were comforting, reliable, and safe. Now that we are older, I take care of you. The touch of your familiar hands helps me cope with your memory loss. I kiss them all the time. As my tears cascade down my cheeks, you tenderly wipe them dry.

Letisha Johnson vs. Joseph Kelly in The Case of The Blinding Smile

Cast of Characters

Perry Mason – fictional defense attorney, won every case he fought on TV. Can he win a real-life case?

James Earl Jones – Spokesman for New Jersey Bell, has a resonant voice. Has pursued people who have switched from NJ Bell to another long-distance phone company, prosecutor

Joseph Wapner – Judge formerly of *People's Court*. Tried another case involving the defendant.

Letisha Johnson – Victim of Joe's blinding smile

Joe "Everyone Calls Me Kelly" Kelly – defendant

JW to Prosecutor: Call your first witness.

JEJ: I call Letisha Johnson.

LJ is sworn in.

JEJ: Ms. Johnson, please describe the events leading up to your blindness.

LJ: I was out walking one afternoon when, all of a sudden, I saw a blinding light. My first reaction was to turn away, but I couldn't; it was as if I was in a trance. My first thought was, it must be a nuclear explosion. My second thought was, has the sun fallen from the sky? Then I thought perhaps it's a UFO. The next day when I awoke, I was blind.

JEJ to Perry Mason: Your witness.

PM to Ms. Johnson: Why weren't you wearing your sunglasses?

LJ: Well, first off, it was the dead of winter with a blinding snowstorm raging at the time. *Pointing to the defendant.* He's a slick one; he's so skinny that when he turned sideways, he disappeared.

PM: Did you see the doctor?

LJ: Yes, he told me he doesn't know if the blindness is temporary or permanent.

Thank you, Ms Johnson, you may step down now.

PM: I call the defendant, "Kelly."

PM to Kelly: Please tell the court your hygienic practices.

JK: As soon as I wake up, I floss and brush my teeth. After I eat, I floss and brush my teeth. After I use the bathroom, I floss and brush my teeth. As a matter of fact, all the money I make at work, I spend on floss, toothpaste, and toothbrushes. So, I guess you could say I have a million-dollar smile.

PM: Thank you, Kelly, you may step down now.

PM: I rest my case.

JEJ: I have a surprise witness.

Everyone in the courtroom gasps after seeing the door open and the nub marching in.

Your honor, I call Mr. Nub to the stand.

Nub sworn in.

JEJ to Mr. Nub: Please tell the court the character of the defendant, Mr. Kelly.

N: This guy is insane, not only did he spend all his time flossing and brushing his teeth, but he also did the same to us his nubs. That's why we were so shiny.

Thank you, Mr. Nub, you may step down now.

Judge to jury: You can find the defendant guilty on one or more of the following offenses: being vain, keeping the toothpaste industry single-handedly in business, assault with a deadly weapon—his teeth, attempted murder. Flossing and brushing his nubs.

Jury to judge: We find the defendant, Joe Kelly, guilty on all charges.

Judge to jury: Please decide his punishment.

Judge to JK: How did you escape the island of tobacco?

JK to judge: I traded my TV for a boat. The people there have never seen reruns of *Gilligan's Island* or *Cool Runnings*.

Jury to judge: We hereby sentence the defendant, Joe Kelly, to a lifetime of poor hygiene. We hereby confiscate all tools used for the care of his teeth, including but not limited to toothpaste, toothbrushes, and floss.

We also sentence him to "get a life"; find another hobby.

JK faces his accuser.

I apologize to Ms. Johnson. My intent was never to blind her but only to get her to notice me. In this, I have failed. Now for the rest of my life I have to live with dingy teeth. Somehow, to me, the punishment doesn't fit the crime.

The End

Part I

Rosa Rodriguez is a vivacious, opinionated reporter with a sense of humor that appeals to her television audience. She has worked for East Coast News for five years. After this interview, she was admitted to the psych ward of Bellevue Hospital. Rhonda LeStinky has decided that bathing is optional. She is responsible for the hospitalization of thousands of people and the inadvertent death of those overcome by her noxious fumes. Her family has disowned her, and all her friends have abandoned this pariah. DA Frank Giordano is a confident professional who always wins his cases. He has never had to deal with the Great Unwashed before this trial. Although he has been a lead prosecutor for twenty-five years, this has so affected his health that he has decided to take an early retirement. Martin Lupino is a legal aid lawyer who has defended the rights of all people no matter their ability to pay. He is a brash, young jokester who suffers from an extremely rare condition known as lack of smell. His nostril nerves were paralyzed in a freak biking accident at age five. After defending this witness, his condition miraculously improved, and he now wears a gas mask wherever he goes. The judge presiding over this case, Matilda Trachtenberg, has been handling civil matters since she graduated from Brooklyn Law School. She is known on the bench as a cool, calm, collected woman. After this trial, she takes a month-long vacation to Calcutta, India, to breathe in the putrid odors of this city. Various character witnesses for the prosecution and the defense.

EXTERNAL: NYC courtroom

Rosa

Hello, everyone. This is Rosa Rodriguez reporting for East Coast News. Our top story of the day: There has been an outbreak of a disease labeled by experts as the Great Unwashed Syndrome. The symptoms are varied and include believing that one, bathing is optional; two, oral hygiene is unnecessary, and three, deodorant should be outlawed. If you experience any of these thoughts, please contact your doctor immediately. We will meet with the first known case of this sordid disease. (Walks over to Rhonda) I'm talking to Rhonda LeStinky. According to her blog, she hasn't bathed in thirty years. (Rosa is overtaken by the stench and almost faints. She holds the microphone at least three feet away from her subject while trying to hold her breath. Rosa spritzes lavendar perfume on Rhonda and herself to mask this stench) Miss LeStinky, why did you decide that good hygiene was unnecessary?

Rhonda

I've always considered bathing optional. My skin was always dry and crusty, and soap and water tended to irritate it. Plus, I want to conserve our natural resources. There are people who actually shower three times a day. Isn't that disgusting? Wasting water is not an option for me. Why don't those same people wash in the ocean?

Rosa

I'm sure that you're aware that there is a large selection of lotions and creams you could use to combat dry skin.

Rhonda

I don't want any chemicals touching my baby-soft bottom. Besides, all of this costs money, and I want to save as much as I can.

Rosa

Unlike in some third-world countries, there is no shortage of clean water. Don't you feel that your breath and armpit malodor might offend some people and cause other folks to vomit?

Rhonda

Actually, if they do upchuck/hurl, it might improve my scent.

Rosa

Miss LeStinky, I heard that there was a class-action lawsuit on behalf of all the people who suffered irreparable damage to their noses, not to mention broken bones from running away from you. How do you feel about your upcoming trial?

Rhonda

I believe that it's a conspiracy on the part of big corporations who manufacture soap, toothpaste, deodorant, etc. They're losing plenty of money on my not purchasing these frivolous items.

Rosa

(Her eyes start watering/tearing; she loses her lunch and begins babbling incoherently. Her flaccid body hits the concrete. Her co-anchor calls for an ambulance, and she is rushed to the hospital where the doctors fill her blackened lungs with pure oxygen and hook her up to a ventilator. Later, she is transferred to the psych ward.)

All rise, Judge Mathilda Trachtenberg presiding over the case number 2765 on the docket for The State of New York versus Rhonda LeStinky.

Frank

(Faces the courtroom filled with curious bystanders.) Ladies and gentlemen of the jury, you may be asking yourselves why we have brought this seemingly innocent and humble senior citizen to court. On the date in question, the population of New York, as well as areas of New Jersey and Connecticut, became aware of a putrid and offensive stench allegedly emanating from 100 Quentin Road, Apt. 1C, in Brooklyn. Was this more-than-offensive odor a broken sewer line? No. Was it a garbage dump? No. Ladies and gentlemen of the jury, we are prepared to prove to you, with the help of expert testimony, beyond a reasonable doubt, that this foul odor was and continues to be none other than Rhonda LeStinky. (Everyone in the courtroom gasps in amazement and disbelief.)

Judge Trachtenberg

Council for the defense, how does your client plead?

Martin

Not guilty, Your Honor. Ladies and gentlemen of the jury, we are prepared to show that Miss LeStinky was the victim of neglect and improper training as a child and whose BO is therefore the direct result of an Aroma Dysfunctional Family, AKA ADF.

Frank

As our first witness, Your Honor, we would like to bring Samantha Stevens, the accused own daughter, to the stand. (Samantha is sworn in.) Please tell the court in your own words what it's like to live with the accused.

Samantha

Well, she never bathes nor brushes her teeth. She wears the same dirty clothes and uses the same dirty bedsheets for weeks or months at a time. She's a bad influence on my children. She tries to kiss me, but the stench and filth she exudes forces me to back away. Otherwise, I fear I will pass out. I think I come close to passing out when I get a whiff of her feet. She never washes her hands after going to the bathroom. I find I can't eat the food she cooks for fear of food poisoning. She produces enough dandruff for skiing on the Swiss Alps.

Martin

Objection, Your Honor. The witness is embellishing her testimony.

Judge Trachtenberg

Objection sustained. Miss Stevens, please just state the facts.

Frank

Are there other siblings, and do they share your sentiments?

Samantha

Yes, and yes.

Frank

How does your mother react when you tell her her BO is offensive?

Samantha

She just laughs and shrugs it off.

Frank

No further questions, Your Honor.

Judge Trachtenberg

(Addresses the defense.) Your witness, council.

Martin

No questions. We request Mrs. LeStinky's friend, Miss Tellitlikeitis, to the stand. (Witness is sworn in.) In your opinion, Miss Tellitlikeitis, what kind of person is Rhonda LeStinky?

Tellitlikeitis

Well, first of all, she's extremely sociable and a true culture vulture. She frequents the latest Broadway shows, movies, and cultural events. She appreciates the art of fine dining and eats out a lot. She's also very active in charitable organizations. She's done a lot for the Brooklyn Heights Orchestra. You'll often see her in the neighborhood fundraising or putting up flyers. She's a true pillar of her community.

Martin

Anything else you'd like to add?

Tellitlikeitis

Yes. Being as active as Rhonda is, she's almost never home.

Martin

So, she would be envied by, let's say, those who don't have much of a life.

Tellitlikeitis

Exactly. That's why her jealous children hate her and would do anything to destroy her. You can't believe a word they say. (Raises voice for emphasis and stands up.) They're just rotten kids.

Frank

I motion Miss Tellitlikeitis's testimony be stricken from the record, Your Honor. She has a long history of playing the devil's advocate.

Judge Trachtenberg

Motion denied.

Frank

As the people's next witnesses, we would like to bring the grandchildren of the accused, Thomas and Tara, to the stand. (Thomas is sworn in.) Please tell the court about Grandma.

Thomas

She smells funny, and her teeth look like doo-doo cocky. She tells Tara and me to eat an apple in the morning like she does, but she still has barf breath. Once, she was cooking spaghetti and was wearing nothing but a bra...

Judge Trachtenberg

That will be quite enough, young man. Please step down now.

(Tara is sworn in.)

Tara

Grandma stinks.

Frank

No further questions.

Judge Trachtenberg

Your witness, council.

Martin

Tara, tell us about the day Grandma was talking to the crossing guard.

Tara

Well, Grandma stopped to have her usual conversation; blah, blah, blah, yadda, yadda, yadda.

Martin

And how close were you when Grandma was talking?

Tara

Very close.

Martin

And how did the crossing guard react to Grandma's alleged bad breath odor?

Tara

She didn't react. She didn't seem to notice that Grandma stinks.

Martin

No more questions. I motion that the taxpayers' money not be wasted any further, Your Honor, and that all charges against Mrs. LeStinky be dropped.

Frank

Not until the court hears from our next witness. The people call to the stand an expert witness, a Doctor of Medicine as well as psychiatry and an expert in SOS. (Doctor sworn in.) Doctor, you heard Tara's testimony. Please explain to the court, in layman's terms, how it is possible that the crossing guard was unaware of Mrs. LeStinky's bad breath?

Doctor

Well, when a person comes into contact with a powerful, malodorous entity like that of Mrs. LeStinky's breath and is subjected to a big whiff of it all at once, their olfactory nerve, the sense responsible for smelling, goes into shock and, in defense to the stench, shuts itself down.

Frank

So, what you're saying is that it is merely a defense mechanism.

Doctor

The crossing guard was a victim of Shock Olfactory Syndrome, as it is known in the medical community, or SOS.

Frank

Could others not reacting to Mrs. LeStinky's BO and bad breath be explained by this phenomenon?

Doctor

Yes, but I'm afraid that her family members' olfactory nerves are subjected to the stench all the time and have therefore built up an immunity to this reaction.

Frank

What professional advice, then, would you give to the family members?

Doctor

None. Just my deepest sympathies.

Frank

No more questions.

Martin

As a doctor of psychiatry, how would you explain why a woman who otherwise functions normally in every other aspect of her life refuses to bathe, wash her hair, brush her teeth, change her clothes, or take any measures toward any kind of physical hygiene? Does this make sense, in your professional opinion?

Doctor

Obviously, something went awry in her psychological development as a child. She most definitely came from an ADF, and emphasis was not placed on physical cleanliness nor was it given priority. This was surely a result of her parents' own upbringing, the availability of fresh water, so on and so forth.

Martin

So, you could say that she was a victim.

Doctor

Yes, I suppose so.

Frank

Request to cross-examine.

Judge Trachtenberg

Go ahead, council.

Frank

Isn't it true that both Mrs. LeStinky's brother and sister maintain a very high standard of physical cleanliness and have done so most of their lives? Isn't it true that Mrs. LeStinky's own offspring bathe regularly, as do all the people she comes into contact with? Isn't it also true that she is surrounded, yes, even bombarded by mental images and messages of physical cleanliness by the society she lives in?

Doctor

(Doctor nods yes to all his questions.)

Frank

How can we continue to excuse Mrs. LeStinky's behavior on the grounds that she is a victim? What about us? Aren't we the victims?

Martin

Objection. Council is badgering the witness.

Judge Trachtenberg

Objection sustained.

Frank

Judge, ladies and gentlemen of the jury, I would like to bring in our most powerful testimony of all. Exhibit number one: Rhonda LeStinky.

Judge Trachtenberg

I must warn all those present. This subject is not intended for those with a weak stomach or those who are especially sensitive to foul odors. (Rhonda LeStinky is brought into the courtroom. Babies cry. Women faint. People gasp for air and try desperately to cover their noses with handkerchiefs or anything they find available.)

Frank

We would like to bring our final witness to the stand. A New York City garbageman of twenty years and the appointed supervisor put in charge of the special detective unit assigned to locating the source of the alleged stench, Mr. Schnozzola. (Witness sworn in.) Mr. Schnozzola, after several days of investigation, would you please indicate to the court what or, rather, who you found to be the source of the hideous odor in question, and what brought you to this conclusion?

Mr. Schnozzola

Well, it was difficult at first because it seemed the odor traveled around the city to various restaurants, movie theaters, etc., and it seemed to permeate everything it came into contact with. Finally, it made an unusual move. We located it at eleven o'clock at night traveling down the middle of a street in Brooklyn. There was Mrs. LeStinky walking in the direction of her house. When we asked her why she was walking in the middle of the street so late at night, she informed us it was so as not to get mugged. As soon as she opened her mouth, we knew that not only was she not going to get mugged, for no mugger would dare come within one hundred feet of her, but that our search was over. She's right there.

Frank

Please note for the record that Mr. Schnozzola pointed to Mrs. LeStinky.

Judge Trachtenberg

The jury will give us their verdict after a short recess.

Jury Foreman

That won't be necessary, Judge. Our verdict is in, and it's unanimous. We find the defendant guilty as charged. We sentence Rhonda LeStinky to take a bath, wash her hair, wash her hands after going to the bathroom, brush her teeth, change her clothes, and change her bedsheets every day for the rest of her life.

Rosa

Hello, everyone. This is Rosa Rodriguez reporting for East Coast News. I was supposed to be covering the trial of the century. But, unfortunately, the fumes from the Rhonda LeStinky interview scrambled my brain cells, and I was involuntarily committed to Bellevue for ten days. My psychiatrist allowed me to use my one-day pass to come to court. I'm here in front of Civil Court on 293 Adams Street. I just found out that Miss LeStinky has been found guilty on all counts. Although the jury didn't recommend any jail time, she was sentenced to clean up her act. There has been worldwide attention drawn to this spectacle. Our sources have indicated that Proctor & Gamble and a host of other large companies have agreed to provide Miss LeStinky with a lifetime of FREE products. They have even agreed to waive the shipping charges. Thanks, FedEx. Thanks for watching. See you next week.

Lousy Service

C1 - Sunny is a twenty-year-old male waiter.

C2 - Bill is a fifty-year-old male customer with a thick Brooklyn accent.

C3 - Jose is a twenty-five-year-old male cook with a thick Spanish accent.

C4 - Betty Sue is a twenty-nine-year-old female waitress with a Southern drawl. She is a former employee of Walmart.

C5 - Catherine is a thirty-year-old female manager.

C6 - Lenny is head of the Seneca Health Department. He moonlights as a refrigerator repairman. (Scene takes place in the All-American Diner one spring day on a Thursday at 1 p.m. Jukebox in the background is blaring "New York, New York." The kitchen and dining area are visible to the audience, with a door separating the two.)

Sunny

Good Afternoon. Welcome to the All-American Diner. My name is Sunny, and I'll be your waiter. (Hands customer a menu.)

Bill

I've never eaten here before, but my wife, Mabel, tells me you got good service and cheap prices. What do you recommend?

Betty Sue

(While cleaning a nearby table, she overhears the conversation and rushes over.) Oh, you have a wife named Mabel, how sweet. My sister's name is Maybelle.

Sunny

(Furiously whispers in her ear.) Why don't you go find your own customer? As I was saying, sir, all the food is exceptional, but I love the roast beef smothered in mushrooms.

Bill

Okay, I'll take that and a cuppa coffee. Does that come with fries?

Sunny

Yes, but you can substitute another vegetable if you like. We have baked potatoes, broccoli, corn, and string beans.

Bill

Nah, I'll just have the fries.

Sunny

(Writes down order and takes back menu.) Very good, sir. Would you like some bread and butter while you're waiting for your meal?

Bill

Yeah. Can you hurry with the order? I'm starving.

Betty Sue

Sir, can I help you with your napkin? I've been doing this for my family ever since I was a youngster. My pa said I was the best napkin tucker in all of South Carolina. (She reaches for the napkin and knocks over the condiments.)

Bill

(Yells.) Lady, get away from me! I can fix my own napkin. And, besides, you're clumsy.

Betty Sue

(Tearfully apologizes.) I'm really sorry. I always try to be helpful to the customers. Most people love my Southern hospitality.

Sunny

(Talking to Bill.) I'll tell the chef to put a rush on it. (Walks back to the kitchen.) Hey, Jose, can you get this cooked fast? The guy in booth seven says he's starving.

Jose

Okay, boss. (Takes ticket from Sunny and begins to slowly read the order aloud.) Tell the guy to order something else. We didn't get the meat delivery today.

Sunny

Why didn't you tell me this when I got to work this morning?

Jose

You didn't ask.

Sunny

(Angrily stomps away from the kitchen. Warily approaches booth seven.) Sir, according to our knowledgeable Chef Jose, we are out of roast beef. Perhaps you'd like to order something else?

Bill

I was just licking my chops, and now you're gonna disappoint me. What else you got?

Sunny

We have some delicious boneless salmon glazed in grape jelly with a side of asparagus.

Bill

Okay, I'll take that. But step on it...my stomach's growling.

Sunny

(Puts the bread basket, butter, and coffee on the table.) Very good, sir. (Walks back to the kitchen.) Jose, please make this as fast as possible. The guy's getting agitated, and I want a good tip.

Jose

(After reading the order, starts to shake his head.) Look in the refrigerator and see if we have any salmon.

Sunny

(Peers into the refrigerator.) It stinks in here. When was the last time you cleaned this out?

Jose

That would be in 1999. I thoroughly scrubbed the inside with a toothbrush dipped in vinegar and baking soda. It took me a whole day. Catherine insisted on it. But since then, I don't smell anything. Of course, I do have a deviated septum.

Catherine

(Walking around with a clipboard, taking an inventory of the food.) Jose, why didn't you tell me we didn't get a meat delivery today? And why are we out of so many ingredients? You know the rule: I deal directly with the vendors. Your job is just to prepare meals. Why is that such a hard thing for you to do?

Jose

Listen, Catherine, I've been working this stupid job for ten years, and you are never going to promote me to head chef. I want a raise.

Catherine

Are you serious? You are the only chef working here.

Sunny

All I see are some wilted vegetables, moss-covered fruit salad, and some unidentified pieces of food particles.

Jose

Check in the freezer. I'm sure I put some fresh fish in there last year. Could be cod or fillet. I don't know.

Sunny

Are you crazy? You can't keep fish for more than a week. Get your butt over here and find the salmon.

Jose

If you don't see it, then we don't have it. Tell him to order something else.

Sunny

(Sweat starts to bead on his forehead.) I'm not going to ask him to order something else. He's a big guy, and the last thing I need is a broken nose. Let's try this again. Why don't you give me an inventory of what we do have?

Jose

Sorry, Sunny, but I don't have time. I have all these other orders piling up. Take your attitude and complaints to the boss.

Sunny

(Face changes shade from white to pink and then an angry shade of red [crimson] and raises voice.) This customer has been waiting awhile to be served. Tell me what we have, then I can give him a choice of our limited supply of food.

Jose

Okay, don't get your boxers in a knot. Give me a second. We have spaghetti, veggie balls, and salad.

Sunny

Great! Now I want you to repeat what you just told me to the guy in booth seven. Capisce? You know, Jose, every day I come to work in this Mickey Mouse outfit, strangling on this red polyester tie. I deal with irate customers and our nasty boss, Catherine. I go home each night smelling of stale grease and dried sweat. But the worst part of my job is dealing with a moron like you. Your IQ is the size of a mustard seed.

Betty Sue

You're always fussing and hollering at each other. You two act like an old married couple. Why, I recall my Aunt Thelma and Uncle Jeb were always yelling at each other, but they always made up after dinner.

Sunny

(Talking to Betty Sue.) You're a ditz. Any time you open that mouth of yours, it sounds like a bad case of diarrhea. I'm just curious; does brain damage run in your family?

Jose

Yeah, well, it isn't all roses working with a guy like you. You have no sense of humor. Okay, chief, I'll tell the guy what we have available.

Sunny

(At the booth.) Sir, I'm sorry for the delay. The chef, Jose, has a selection of dishes he can prepare for you.

Bill

What the hell is going on here? This place came highly recommended, and you people act like this is a skit from *Abbott and Costello*.

Jose

Sir, we are a high-class diner who usually serves the low-class riff raff from downtown. Hoity toity is our claim to fame. This is what we got available for today. Spaghetti, veggie balls, and garden salad. What is your pleasure, sir?

Bill

Give me the spaghetti and veggie balls and make it snappy.

Sunny

Because you've been so patient about the mix-up, we are giving you a dessert at no charge.

Jose

(Walks to kitchen to prepare meal. Clanking noises.) Sunny, pick up for table seven.

Sunny

Thanks, Jose. Sir, would you like a refill on your coffee?

Bill

Sure, why not? Apparently, I'll need to stay awake long enough to enjoy my meal.

Sunny

(Picks up order.) Here you go, sir.

Bill

(Closely examines his food.) Isn't this interesting? Since when do veggie balls have mice tails? And why is there cigarette ash on my spaghetti? What is a dead roach doing floating in my coffee? I'm sure the health department would be interested in these exotic additives in the food.

Sunny

(Horrified expression. Yells.) Jose, you're fired! This time the health department is sure to close us down. You can't bribe your way out of this mess.

Catherine

You have no authority to fire Jose. I don't even have that authority. When did the health department show up? Did we ever get a summons? I'm in charge, and no one tells me anything. This place is worse than a circus.

Jose

(Laughs.) That's why they call me the creative cook.

(Bill jumps up, overturning the table, and storms out of the restaurant muttering incoherently. After exiting the diner, he reaches for his cell phone and starts dialing.)

Catherine

Everyone, in the kitchen, now! I'm calling a meeting. (Sunny, Jose, and Betty Sue follow Catherine into the kitchen.) Okay, we have to clean this place up. We're going to pull an all-nighter. Call your other halves and tell them that they won't be seeing you again until tomorrow.

Sunny

Are you kidding? It'll take weeks to straighten this mess out.

Betty Sue

Oh, Sunny, don't be so negative. I'm sure if we all pitch in together, we can get the diner in tiptop shape. I recall that when I was working in Walmart, the customers would throw the clothing all over the place. We were able to pick up, fold, and replace it by 9 p.m. every night. Selma Jean would do an inspection, and she always praised our team spirit. Gee, I miss working there. Being underpaid was the highlight of my career. If I'd stayed there, I could've at least been an assistant manager by now. (Looking pensive.)

Jose

Hey, Betty Sue, do you think you could hook me up with a job there? Anything is better than working at this place.

Sunny

Catherine, I think you're an incompetent manager. This place has been going downhill, and you've had your head buried in that stupid clipboard of yours. I've been basically standing in for you, and I'm sick of it.

Catherine

Sunny, get off your high horse. If we don't pass inspection this time, they'll close the diner down for good. We'll all be unemployed. Betty Sue, I want you to put the closed sign on the door. I'm going to assign each of you specific tasks. Don't argue with me because we don't have much time. And, remember, I intend on doing a quick scan after everyone finishes. (After giving instructions, everyone scatters. They race around looking for spackle, paint, cleaning supplies and furiously start working.)

Scene Two: It's 9 a.m. on Friday in the kitchen. Everyone is sitting around, exhausted, yawning with bloodshot eyes. Catherine is frantically going around checking everyone's work.

Catherine

Okay, everything looks decent. I think we can get by this time. We'll do a thorough cleaning after the inspection. Betty Sue, I want you to unlock the door but keep the closed sign up.

Lenny

(Lights out. Lights up. The next day. Casually strolls into diner and looks around.) Well, I see things haven't changed much since I was here a week ago. Chaos still reigns supreme.

Catherine

I didn't call you. The refrigerator is still working. What are you doing here anyway?

Lenny

Oh, don't you know? I recently got a job with the health department. I'm in my official capacity as an inspector.

Catherine

Lenny, can you please give us a moment? (Everyone heads to the kitchen.)

Lenny

Sure, no problem. (Sits in booth.)

Catherine

(Gives orders in an authoritative tone.) Betty Sue, since you're our secret weapon, I want you to flirt with Lenny. Say and do whatever is necessary to keep him busy for a few minutes. Give him anything he wants gratis...that means free. Keep refilling his coffee cup and give him as many slices of the homemade apple pie as he wants.

Betty Sue

(At the booth.) Hi, Lenny. I just want you to know that you are the most attractive man I've ever seen. How about after work you take me out? We could go to the bar, and afterwards, you can come to my place.

Lenny

I don't think my wife, Tracy, would like that. She's not the understanding type. Enough of your stalling. I need to get on with the inspection. I have another one in about an hour, and I don't want to be late. (Points to his watch for emphasis.)

Betty Sue

I know I've been jawing, but I find you so attractive. You have such thick red hair. I've never seen that particular shade on a man before. I want to run my fingers through your dandruff encrusted hair. (Proceeds to put her hand on his head.)

Lenny

No, Betty Sue, stop that, wait. No one touches my hair except my wife Tracy.

Betty Sue

(Gets ring caught on toupee. Slowly lifts it off Lenny's head fascinated. Then starts screaming and running toward kitchen.) Somebody help me, I got a rat caught on my finger.

Lenny

(Jumps up and starts chasing Betty Sue. Yelling.) Come back with my hair, you idiot.

Catherine

What's all the commotion? Betty Sue, stop screaming this minute. (Grabs hold of her elbow and puts her in nearest chair.)

Betty Sue

(Holds her hand up while the toupee dangles helplessly.) I was just trying to help. Then I got carried away and started to run my fingers through his thick thatch of red hair. My ring got caught in his hairpiece, and I panicked. Catherine, please help me get this rug off of my ring.

Lenny

(An enraged and breathless Lenny catches up to Betty Sue.) Give me back my toupee this instant. I spent thousands of dollars getting it, and you're ruining it with your stupid ring. You are the most incompetent waitress I've ever dealt with in my life.

Catherine

Lenny, I'm so sorry. Just give me a minute and I will untangle your toupee. I will personally pay for any damages to your hairpiece. (Hands Lenny the toupee. Walks with Lenny back to the dining area.)

Lenny

I'm just trying to do my job. How much longer do I have to wait until the inspection?

Catherine

Just five more minutes. Can I bring you anything else to eat?

Lenny

(Sits down.) No, I'm full.

Catherine

Okay, Lenny, you can go and do your inspection. I think you'll be surprised at the outcome.

Lenny

I came prepared for this diner to fail the inspection. After all, I'm an eyewitness to the filth that covers everything. And let's not mention the rodents that have a party every night. (Thoroughly checks out the kitchen area. He first goes to the refrigerator and opens it. Jose is standing in there like a statue, shivering. Lenny is so shocked, he jumps back and falls down.) Jose, what the hell are you doing in there?

Jose

Freezing my ass off. No, just kidding. I got stuck in here last night. I forgot to put the wedge in the door. Sorry if I scared you, but I've been banging on this door for hours. (Helps Lenny to his feet.)

Lenny

(Walks into the refrigerator.) This icebox is almost empty. Where is all the food? What is this green stuff? Hey, it looks like fungus. And what's on the floor? It's sticky and greasy,

Catherine

(Whispers into Jose's ear.) I thought you cleaned it. You said you were in there all night. What were you doing then?

Jose

I was shivering. It was too cold to clean, and besides, I was tired, so I guess I took a little nap.

Lenny

This doesn't look good. I hope the rest of the place is in order. (Walks to the grill and starts inspecting it. Runs his fingers along the metal.) This is filthy. It looks like there is years of accumulation of dust. When was the last time this was cleaned?

Sunny

It was wiped down recently. (Sunny looks at the filthy rags and then realizes he was cleaning with dirt.)

Lenny

(Carefully examines the floor.) These look like rodent droppings. Betty Sue, is that a rat near your foot?

Betty Sue

(She pushes the rat back through the large hole in the wall.) Why no, I don't see any varmints here. Maybe you need to get some eyeglasses.

Lenny

(He touches the freshly painted walls.) What is this? Grease. How does grease get on fresh paint?

Catherine

I think you're mistaken. Jose didn't cook anything yet. So maybe that's some other substance.

Lenny

Why is Sunny leaning against the wall? It looks like that wallpaper is about to glide off the walls.

Sunny

Well, you could say that I was holding the paper up until it dries.

Lenny

(Continues the inspection. After about an hour of writing down all the violations, he is through.) Catherine, this place is a dismal failure. This notice will stay on the door until all the violations are corrected and the fines paid. I can't believe people actually eat at this rodent-infested place. This is the nastiest place I've ever inspected.

Catherine

Well, guys, I guess we can all go out for drinks since we won't we working for a long, long time.

The end.

Children of the Night

Crack! Crack! Crack! The distinctive sound of gunfire caught our attention. We were poised to flee the whizzing bullets piercing the night's silence. Overhead hung the acrid residue of gunpowder that stung our youthful noses. The glowing full moon illuminated the floating particles. In unison, we dropped to the grass-covered lawn and crawled to the safety of our abode. As they pursued us with exaggerated zeal, we overheard their whispered plan to exterminate our footprints from the surface of the earth.

I walked on the campus of the College of Staten Island in late January. I was drawn toward the sound of trickles of water in a metal barrel on its side, surrounded by concrete. As I gazed at my reflection in a nearby puddle, I clearly saw my six feet, five inches of pure blubber. My etched leather belt was ostensibly doing a good job of holding up my enormous belly. My favorite Wrangler jeans were pockmarked with various-shaped holes. My red and blue checkered shirt had seen better days. I was ready to spring for new suspenders since the ones I was wearing were ready for the landfill. My scuffed, size-thirteen black square-toed Durango cowboy boots were proudly worn as a badge of honor. I completed my western ensemble with my grey ten-gallon hat arrayed with colorful eagle feathers. The realization that, at fifty, I was in the worst shape of my life hit me square in the gut. The *Biggest Loser* beckoned me.

I turned my attention to the flurry of runaway children racing toward their hiding place. Holding my trusty notebook and my lucky yellow pen, I cautiously approached them. Our eyes met, and a slow smile spread across my ruddy face. The children froze, uncertain if I was friend or foe. I shouted out, "Mangellan Crawford." Their bodies relaxed, and they ushered me into their world.

"Hey guys, I'm here to interview you for the article we spoke about on the phone." They quickly gathered around me like ants to a picnic spread. I looked them over and noticed the disparity in their sizes. The kids were of various ethnic groups, yet they appeared as a united throng. The one who I gathered was probably their leader, the tall, lanky one with the unruly brown hair, began to speak.

"Mr. Crawford, I'm glad that you decided to show up. We have contacted other reporters, but they weren't interested in speaking to us," said the leader.

My pen hovered over the pad ready to write the article. "I was intrigued by your story. Please introduce me to your friends," I prodded.

"This here is Red. We've been pals for about a year." He gently coaxed his friend to shake my hand. "Woolley joined our gang about six months ago. We found Cherry sleeping in a dumpster. Basil is our lookout guard."

"You all seem to have unusual names," I observed. "Are they your birth names?"

"Nah, I made them up. We have to be careful—most adults are our enemies. Red is named for his red hair, and he has lots of freckles. Woolley has hair like steel wool. Basil always smells like the herb, and Cherry has bright red cheeks."

That made such logical sense to me that I had to commend him for his creativity. "You're sure a smart guy. What do you call yourself?"

"Chestnut, because I love eating 'em."

I looked at this mélange of youngsters. As I inched closer, the odor became unbearable. The stench of unwashed bodies mingled with the smell of smeared feces permeated their threadbare clothes and was enough to make me want to retch. Instead, I had a coughing fit. I endured this because I had promised this eager bunch of children that I would expose the circumstances of their predicament.

"Chestnut, how did you find me?" I asked.

"I read about you in the *Advance*. You write wonderful articles, and you seem to care about the underdog. I called the newspaper, and they gave me your contact information."

"Thanks for your vote of confidence. I believe that compassion never goes out of style," I said. "Okay, now what do you want to expose about the police department?"

"First off, are you wired? Is this conversation being recorded?" he asked.

"You're mighty suspicious. I do have a Sony voice-activated tape recorder in my pocket. With your permission, I would like to tape this conversation." I did this as a precaution so that I had proof that I was not making up these stories. Chestnut noded his agreement. These kids appeared to be innately intelligent. I assessed their ages to be between ten and fifteen years. I turned on my machine and began asking the questions. I had to be careful because they feared authority figures.

Chestnut took a deep breath and began. "Like I said, we're from different backgrounds. Red is Irish, and he and his family like to drink. One time, his old man went on a drunken binge, broke a wine bottle, and cut him on his forehead. The cut's gone, but he's still messed up. Cherry, I think she's German or something, became a prostitute. Her sister got her into it, needed money to pay loan sharks. Cherry ran away one night, and that's when we found her. Woolley, the black dude, was living with his uncle, Tex. One night, Tex decided to join him in his bed. His uncle wanted some sex, and when Woolley refused, Tex beat him up real bad and then kicked him out of the house. Basil, who's Arab, got adopted from Russia. He never felt like he was a part of the family. Eventually, he got thrown out because he screwed around with his stepsister. His parents freaked out. I am the token white guy. I grew up in Tottenville. When I was fourteen, my dad bailed. Mom said he just abandoned us, but I didn't believe her since we were tight, and he would never leave without telling us. The cops were suspicious, too. They later found his body wrapped up in a rug in the trunk of his car. Mom wanted to hook up with her boyfriend because he wasn't gonna wait."

I was speechless. "I'm so sorry," I said, then continued, "How did you find this place?"

"At first we were living in Willowbrook Park. But there was no shelter. We had fun, though. Fed the ducks and took turns riding the carousel, thanks to a generous lady who felt sorry for us and paid for our tickets. We snuck over to the college. They have all these small brick houses scattered throughout the campus. I busted a window, and we climbed inside. It's cold inside but much colder outside. We huddle together for warmth."

"How do you eat?"

"We have a banquet every night. The school throws away tons of leftovers. We eat burgers, pizza, fried chicken, lots of vegetables, fruits—you name it."

"So, you're doing okay, considering..."

"We survive. The problem is the cops. Someone reported us, and they came to investigate. One night, as we were chowing down on some pizza, Red heard a noise. We saw the cops sneaking around and hid. We heard them whispering that their lieutenant wanted them to shoot us like rats and dispose of our bodies. They said he got the idea from an article he read about how the police kill street kids in Brazil."

"I don't believe it. I've always held the police in high regard and respected them immensely," I said. "I have sources in the police department, so I'll check it out. Did you get the name of either the lieutenant or the other officers?"

"Yeah. It's Lieutenant Manning. The other cops just used their last names, Palooka and Marstan."

"Could you describe their attributes?"

"Attributes?"

"What did they look like?"

"It was dark. We hid in the water tunnel. I can recognize their voices. They sounded like they were from Brooklyn. This whole thing makes me very angry. I know you don't believe me, but whatever, we'll deal with it. No way they're gonna throw us out like the rest of the garbage."

"Hey guys, don't give up." I gathered them around me and gave them a hug. The foul smell emanating from these orphans was overpowering my logic. Then, an idea came to me. "Do me a favor and give me everyone's clothing sizes. When I return, I'll bring you new clothes. Is there a place you can bathe?"

"We can soak in the water tunnel. Can you bring us some soap? Make it non-scented; I have allergies to perfume," Chestnut joked, and we all laughed.

"By the way, how did you first phone me?"

"Woolley stole a cell phone from someone in Financial Aid."

"I'm going to give you my cell phone number." I keyed it into the stolen phone. "I'll be in touch."

After leaving them, I drove into the city. I called my source, Dan Midland, gave scant details, and waited for a call back. I've known Dan for about twenty years. We first met when I was covering a homicide. He was one of the investigating officers. I had some inside information about how the crime was committed, and Dan asked me to withhold it for a few days. I complied, and we have been helping each other ever since.

I didn't have to wait long. Apparently this band of ragamuffins wasn't kidding. Dan verified everything. He found out that the top brass had decided it would be more expedient to murder kids than pay to educate, house, and feed them. It was funny; I looked at the police the same way I used to look at criminals. I immediately went home to my messy, unkempt brownstone on West 72nd Street. I searched under a pile of freshly laundered clothing, grabbed my MacBook, and started typing the story that would blow the cover on this sick scheme. I emailed it to my boss, Jim Brady.

He phoned me and asked, "Did you double check your facts? I don't want any problems with the police."

I told him, "There's no reason to. I trust my sources implicitly."

This story hit the newsstand, and all hell broke loose. It ran on the front page. The publicity generated from it was tremendous. The outpouring of rage was phenomenal. The public demanded the ouster of the crooked cops. The mayor then initiated an internal investigation. The little rascals were hailed as heroes. They were eventually adopted by an elderly philanthropist and his adoring younger wife. All the rug rats underwent intensive therapy to deal with the trauma and its aftermath. I was glad that I was able to help these kids.

A few months later, I received a letter, dated October 23, 2008, from my good buddy Chestnut.

Dear Mange,

I want to thank you for everything you've done for us. I'm working hard in school. Although I like Mr. Bland, I hate his wife, Victoria. She's a pervert, and every chance she gets, she rubs up against my privates trying to get a reaction. She coyly whispers in my ear about my rock-hard body, and one time, when I was asleep, she slid into my bed almost naked, except for a see-through teddy. Her flirting is annoying, but Mr. Bland doesn't seem to notice any of her shenanigans. He's nearing eighty and can hardly see anything. I was thinking, perhaps I can live with you, since you don't have any family. I'm miserable here with this sex-crazed bitch. Everyone else is happy since they get whatever they want. Please help me. Chestnut.

After reading his plea for help, I slowly reached for my phone and dialed his number. "Hello, may I please speak to Chestnut

Mall Madness

My husband, Cal, always tells me to rein in my spending. Mostly, I tune him out. His job is to make the money, and mine, of course, is to spend it. Our Saturdays consist of my devoted hubby, who rises at 7 a.m., jumping into the shower and brushing his teeth. He puts on his tattered, slime green terry cloth robe and then brews the morning coffee. He also makes the most delicious banana, chocolate chip pancakes I've ever eaten in my life.

I have a more leisurely approach. I rise at 10 a.m., stretch my lithe limbs, and slowly head to my spacious bathroom. My bare feet touch the heated navy-blue Italian marble tiles. I reach for my Sonic electric toothbrush and glop on some of my Nature's Gate licorice toothpaste. While brushing, I check my face for wrinkles. If I find any, I will immediately make an appointment to get Botox injections. Afterwards, I jump into my Kohler shower and push a button. I am sprayed with pulsating jets of hot, filtered water. I lather up my Cher-length black hair with my pricey Bloomingdale's shampoo and foam up my body with Lush liquid soap. I dry off with my imported, green Egyptian cotton towel. After blow-drying my long locks, I carefully choose an outfit from my extensive collection of Saks Fifth Avenue clothing. I expertly apply my Clinique cosmetics. As I gaze into my full-length mirror, I am reminded what a gorgeous woman I am. I look pretty darn good for a forty-three-year-old. I love being 5'7", and I still wear a size four. My tan skin brings out the deep color of my sea-green eyes.

Then I walk down my fiery red wool-carpeted steps and join my husband for breakfast.

"Hi, honey. Want some coffee and pancakes?"

"Sure, sweetie." I fold my fingers around the steaming white ceramic mug emblazoned with screaming red letters that read "Cincinnati Reds" and dig into the flapjacks with gusto. "Yum, this coffee tastes so good. It's wonderful drinking this on a cold December morning. What are you reading?"

"The usual bad news." Then he says, "Listen, honey, I've got something important to discuss with you."

"Wonderful, darling, but can you at least put the newspaper down while we're having this serious discussion?" I was daintily picking at my pancakes.

Cal has let himself go. His once black hair is studded with strands of gray. His physique was rock hard, but the gym is the last place I can find him. His expanded waistline is evident from his love of food. My strong, robust 6'4" husband, with his beautiful brown eyes, has developed love handles.

"No can do. I'm quite capable of multitasking," he says as he turns to the next page of the newspaper.

I tap my well-manicured nails on the heavy glass oval dining room table. I notice a collection of dust hibernating in the filigree, wrought-iron legs of the table. "Remind me to tell Tessa to clean this area. It looks as if she skipped over it way too long. Anyway, honey, can you speed up this talk? I want to get my nails done before 3 p.m. today."

Cal reluctantly lowers his newspaper and focuses all his attention on me.

"Terri, I happen to know that your spending is out of control. I am well aware that you try to hide the evidence. That shoebox under the bed is overflowing with little white pieces of paper. Also, as you know, I pay all of the bills. I gasped the last time I opened our credit card statement. We owe thousands to American Express. Therefore, I've decided to cut up all your credit cards. I'm going to give you a choice—either you can get a full-time job and start clipping coupons or this sham of a marriage is over. The Sunday paper contains an array of coupons that usually end up in the trash. No more. With Tammy and Jason still in college, we need to be able to pay for their education, which I consider way more important than you buying another pair of Manolo Blahnik shoes," he bellows. "Terri, I want you to know the circumstances behind our marriage. My father and your dad were business rivals. Although they were fierce competitors, they admired each other tremendously."

"What does that have to do with our marriage?" I say looking confused.

"Please don't interrupt. Just listen. When I was at Harvard majoring in business, Clay showed up unexpectedly one weekend at my dorm. He sat me down and told me he had a proposition to make. Apparently, you were such a spoiled diva that he feared you would end up a spinster. I was given the opportunity to woo you; and if I won your hand, I got the prize, a lucrative position at Creative Ads working alongside your dad. At first, I was horrified by this offer, but then I decided, what the heck, I love challenges."

The illusion of my once perfect marriage began to crumble. I am livid. "You mean this was all prearranged? My father would never trade his precious daughter to advance your career," I empathically state. How dare he lie to me? "Liar," I hiss. My feelings are in shreds. I tear the pancakes with my fork.

"If you don't believe me, call him. Clay never lies." He picks up the amber-colored receiver and abruptly handed it to me.

My tears smudge my make-up, and my skin turns an ugly shade of red. I whisper into the phone. "Hello Daddy, it's Terri." I sniffle into the receiver. "Cal and I just had a terrible argument. He told me you would only hire him on the condition that he married me. Tell me this is untrue."

"Sorry, princess, but he's telling you the unvarnished truth. It was a great business deal where we all won." Then his voice turns tender and compassionate before he says, "I made Cal promise never to tell you. Warn the schmuck that he's on the verge of being fired for hurting your feelings."

"I can't believe I was a pawn in this sick game of yours." I whimper. "How dare you gamble with my future. I quit Ball State University for this. I could have been the next Pollock." I then slam the receiver into the hook. I collapse into the nearest brocaded chair. My whole life is in shambles. The house is utterly quiet. The only sound we heard is the antique German cuckoo clock ticking.

"Cal, I want a divorce. I'm sure I'll get most of the stuff in the settlement."

I hear his intake of breath before he continues to obliterate my former happiness.

"Now, honey, please calm down. I'm sorry I blurted out that unkind remark. Although at first our marriage was based on a lie, I do love you. Let's try and resolve this in a calm manner."

"Are you serious? You always said that I was your trophy wife. You promised I would never have to work as long as I took care of the house and the kids. Your colleagues raved about my home-cooked meals when we've entertained them. I've kept up my bargain. Why all of a sudden do you want to limit my spending? I consider this a kind of therapy, retail therapy. Isn't there another way?" I plead.

The wall clock starts to chime at 1 p.m. Sammy, the white Persian cat, jumps onto my lap eagerly awaiting his daily petting.

I hate this man. He's such a cheapskate. Twenty-three years together and this is how he repays my loyalty. Tears began coursing down my cheeks.

Cal continues to speak to me as if I was an indulgent child. He is so condescending.

"There is no other way. I was talking to our accountant, and he advised me that I needed to save more money for our retirement. I'll be forty-five in another two weeks, and I want to add more money to my 401k before I retire in about ten years. You know I love my job at Creative Ads, but once I reach my fifties, your dad will be pressuring me to retire. The company is looking for fresh faces."

I suddenly feel faint. Beads of sweat start to appear on my upper lip. It feels as if my heart will burst. Change is so difficult for me to grasp. I take a good look around at all the nice things we have. I never bought anything on sale. I always paid full price. Then a moment of inspiration strikes.

"Cal, I have a great idea. As you were perusing the *Cincinnati Herald*, I noticed a full-page ad on the back of the paper. There is a new airline, and their prices are dirt cheap. Would you let me have one last shopping spree? I've never been to the Mall of America. I hear that it's the largest Mall in America, located in St. Paul, Minnesota. I promise, after this I will religiously clip coupons and scan supermarket sale sheets for bargains. Agreed?"

Turning the newspaper over, Cal spies the full-page color advertisement. As he reads, his face breaks into a big smile. He looked ten years younger.

"Now you're talking my language. Okay, when do you want to go on this jaunt? I can take my vacation now, but first I have to clear it with my boss. So, give me the dates and I'll speak to him Monday morning."

We run some errands, and of course, I have my nails expertly done at Gloria's Salon.

After conferring with his boss, Cal is given a one-week vacation. I book the tickets and the hotel over the internet. Dana, my next-door neighbor, agreed to look after our cat and take in our newspapers and mail. We leave on December 6th. We check our bags in at the terminal and obtain our boarding passes. We wait in the airport lounge where I nervously down a margarita with relish. Everything seems to be going our way, but I guess there's no such thing as smooth sailing on a cut-rate airline. After entering the smallest plane I've ever been on, we get the shock of our lives.

"Good afternoon, folks. Welcome to Cheapo Air. I will be your captain for Flight 506. My name is Guy Gerard, and my co-pilot's name is Frank Palumbo. We will be departing Cincinnati at 3 p.m. and arriving in St. Paul, Minnesota, at 5 p.m. The temperature in Cincinnati is currently a balmy 30 degrees. The temperature in St. Paul at the moment is a frigid 15 degrees. We will be flying at an altitude of thirty-two thousand feet. Our motto here is, 'We fly on a wing and a prayer.' I hope everyone aboard has taken out an accident insurance policy at the airport."

I look around at the panicked expressions dotting the other passengers' faces and was about to rush off the plane when the captain came on again laughing.

"Just kidding, folks. Since this is a discount airline, we don't employ any flight attendants. No snacks will be served. Please read your safety guidelines just in case we run into any problems. On behalf of myself and my co-pilot, relax and enjoy your flight."

We sit stiff as boards. I am terrified that this tin can of an airplane will fall apart and we will have an untimely death. Cal holds my hand throughout this seemingly endless flight and keeps trying to reassure me that we will make it safely there. The captain attempts to fly a figure eight. During this unexpected feat, I scream, faint, and am out for about an hour. Our seatmate, George, jumps out of his seat and rushes to the cockpit. He bangs so hard on the door that the pilot stops his antics immediately. I find out later that Mr. Gerard was a pilot in the air force and used to perform high altitude stunts to the amusement of the civilians. After a near death scare, we decide that there is no way in hell we are going to get on that plane again. So, we cancel our return flight and book on Delta Airlines.

After arriving at the Holiday Inn, we go to our room to relax. The room is small, with a bunch of cheesy art prints hanging on every wall. The décor is shabby chic. It was the kind of modest room that fit Cal's budget. I take a much-needed nap, and Cal turns on the TV to listen to the news. We dine in the Vecera Restaurant. I splurge and order an Angus hamburger with fries, and Cal orders the shrimp scampi with a side salad. Alcohol flowed easily that night since my nerves were still raw from the crazy airplane ride.

"Cal, I can't wait until tomorrow. I will try and control myself at the mall and not spend all our savings," I jokingly announce to my sourpuss husband.

"Very funny, Terri. We can do some window shopping. Remember, you don't have to buy everything you see, capisce?"

The next morning, the sun makes a rare appearance. I dress quickly, and we take the hotel van to the mall. I am in shopping heaven. They have every store imaginable and then some. We walk arm and arm and slowly explore every crevice of this magnificent place. I feel that we are on our second honeymoon. I spy Nordstrom and rush into the store.

"I've got to get these," I loudly proclaim as I purchase the navy-blue, suede, rabbit-fur-lined gloves and a red-checkered cashmere scarf. Cal smiles and indulges me in my whim.

I think long and hard about what I plan on doing once we return home. I decide that I will begin looking for a job in sales since I love to shop so much. The discounts are fantastic for employees. As for using coupons, that is another matter altogether.

SORE

I was known as the practical joker of Park Slope. One of my most memorable gags involved dog poop placed in a brown paper bag. I put it in front of someone's door, set the bag on fire, and then I rang the doorbell, ran like hell, and hid so I could observe their reaction after they stomped out the fire. Hilarious—until I was grounded for about a month—then not so funny.

I had always wondered why my parents named me Limelight; although with my outgoing personality and the fact that I loved the spotlight, the name is apropos. Even as I matured, I still participated in this craziness.

One day I picked up my landline and called my best friend, Chicky. We've known each other since grade school. I was always the outgoing clown while Chicky was the shy, withdrawn one. We complemented each other's personalities. I was so full of myself that day. I let the phone ring about three times before I heard her soft, melodic voice saying the required greeting.

"Hi, Chicky speaking. How may I help you?"

"Hey, it's Limey. I can't wait to tell you what I've been up to," I excitedly said.

"Please don't. My life has been pretty boring, and I'd like to keep it that way. And besides, every time you come up with those stupid schemes of yours, you always manage to oy vey every Ethel of Brooklyn," she added.

"Oh, come on. You need some excitement to spruce up your dusty life. I'm just the one to give it to you. Anyways, I put this ad on Craigslist in the Community Board section. People can be so foolish. PETA has quite a following of kooks protecting the rights of all kinds of animals, and this got me to thinking. This idea has been brewing in my mind for awhile. I recently saw a billboard for PETA, and I decided to start my own organization. Why don't I organize a demonstration in support of roaches' rights?" I asked enthusiastically.

"Okay, tell me what you put in the ad," she said resignedly.

"I'm going to read it off the internet. Give me a minute for my computer to boot up. Okay here goes: 'According to the *Journal of Entomology*, roaches have been considered a nuisance and a plague since before the beginning of civilization. I wholeheartedly disagree with the *Journal's* assessment. Roaches are, in fact, our children's best friends. The most precious commodity we have. They outnumber humans and singlehandedly hold up our walls. Therefore, I propose that we have a rally in the Times Square area near the TKTS booth on Saturday, August 16, 2008, at 3:00 p.m. Each person who participates and donates at least twenty dollars will receive the coveted SORE T-shirt, which is an acronym that stands for "Save Our Roaches from Extinction." Please invite your friends and relatives to join us on this lifesaving day in history. PETA supports this cause and will have a share in this event. Any money raised will be used exclusively to preserve the short lifespan of our dear friends. If interested in attending this event, call Limelight at (917) 596-9850.'"

"Are you crazy? Who's going to spring for the T-shirts? Do you really think people are that naïve? I've never heard of anyone campaigning for roach rights. Everyone I know, including myself, hates those nasty, brown shiny, winged creatures. I think you need to get yourself a hobby. This is the most outlandish idea you've ever come up with, and I'll have no part of it," she uttered. "Plus, you're almost eighteen, and you still act like a kid. When are you going to grow up?"

"Actually, I think it's a great idea. My Uncle Sid owns a T-shirt company, and I'm sure he'll be glad to supply the clothes at cost. We can use the money we collect to buy new threads. And just so you know, there are people who live in other countries who love to eat these crunchy critters as snacks," I snidely responded. "And besides, I've got the Peter Pan complex. I'll never grow up."

"I bet you don't get even one reply. Prove me wrong and I'll personally hand out the T-shirts to your demonstrators."

"You're on. Plus, you have to agree to wear one of my fabulously designed T-shirts. I'm going to Uncle Sid's factory on Lispenard Street right now to put in an order. I'll make sure I get a variety of sizes. I certainly don't want to exclude children." I laughed.

"Keep me updated on the response you get. I'm going with Melody to Jersey City. I love shopping at the Newport News Mall. I need a new pair of Adidas. Speak to you soon. Bye."

After I spoke with Chicky, I was really sad that she didn't want to help me with my silliness. Every time she participated in my schemes, we always ended up having lots of giggles and telling our friends what stupid stunts we did.

I rummaged around for my money. I had saved $712.50 over the years babysitting all the precious little darlings in my apartment building. I was such a mess. I found coins in my jacket pockets, bills stuffed in my mahogany dresser, and change in my polka dot ceramic piggy bank that my parents gave me when I was ten. After collecting all of this, I took the B train to Grand Street. I phoned my uncle with my trusty red Blackberry and told him what I was up to. Of course, he was agreeable to helping me. After the call, I turned my phone to the silent mode.

"Hi, Uncle Sid," I enthusiastically greeted him. He offered me his best bear hug, and I pleaded for mercy. "You're killing me. I can't breathe," I whined.

He slowly released me and said, "Limey, I've missed you. I never hear from you until you need my services. Do you really think this harebrained idea of yours will work?"

"You bet. People are basically followers. They don't have an original idea in their pea brains. Just look at all those celebrities who tout fashion. They have no sense of flair, yet people buy into this fallacy so easily. I, of course, make up my own style, although I don't have copycats yet." I proudly modeled my outfit of mismatched colors and stretch pants to my uncle. "But eventually the sleepyheads will wake up and see what original outfits I wear, and I'll be the talk of New York," I confidently replied.

"It's funny. I was just thinking about you when you were about five months old. You were trying to say "Mama" in your cute baby babble, and little saliva bubbles kept escaping from your rosebud lips. That was the moment I nicknamed you Bubbles. You still have that bubbly personality." A smile escaped his handsome face as he fondly recalled this.

"Well, Uncle Sid, I'm no longer that small child but a blossoming young woman. Do you perhaps have a photo of that precious Kodak moment?" I eagerly inquired.

"As a matter of fact, I do." He reached into his pocket and pulled out his chubby, black leather wallet. He slowly removed the three rubber bands that were holding it together. After rifling through it for about five minutes, he pulled out a crinkled, faded black-and-white photo of me with my mouth opened and what looked like a transparent globe frozen in place. I gently took the precious keepsake from him and gazed at it. I guess I was a cute little baby after all, with my puffy cheeks and almost bald head. I handed it back to him, and he inserted it into his shrine.

"Do you have any sketches of the design you want on the shirts? Or is this just off the top of your pretty head?" he asked.

Funny, he would have referred to me as pretty. I had never been attractive. My dry, damaged short blonde hair kept me in those awful shellac products for years. My pizza acne had left my face with a perpetual red tint. My thick glasses made me look like a nerd. But I intended on getting the eight-ball contacts so I would look like a cool fool.

"I already know what I want. Capital letters running down the length of the shirt. Just like this." I grabbed a piece of white paper and started to print. "Plus, I want the roach antennas on top of the O. Can you put a picture of a giant roach underneath the lettering?"

"No problem. What color do you want the shirts to be? I have an array of colors that you can choose from if need be."

"White should do it. I also need the information about where the protest will be... I'll need about a hundred to start with, various sizes, and if I need more, I'll call you. How long will it take?"

"Give me about a week. I'm swamped right now with orders from the Diabetes Foundation who are looking to do walks. I'll give it to you at my cost. I need at least half the amount before I begin—a deposit of $250.00."

I couldn't believe he would ask me for a deposit. He's known me all my life. Oh well, I guess business is business.

"Uncle, don't you trust your favorite niece? You know I'm good for the money."

"Limey, when dealing with relatives or customers, I always like to make it an official business deal."

I peeled off the bills and handed them to him. He counted the money and wrote me out a receipt. I scribbled down the rest of the instructions for the shirts. After I exited his store, I happily skipped away, confident that I had messages on my cell phone waiting to be returned.

I walked over to City Hall Park and checked for them. I was right; there were twenty. After listening to all of them, I started to return calls.

Suddenly, I looked up and saw the cutest sight. A fat squirrel was chomping on a banana skin. I always thought those cute furry guys preferred acorns, but I guess their diets are as crappy as humans. This task took me quite some time to finish, and I was starving. It was lunchtime, and I hadn't even eaten breakfast. I spotted one of those yellow umbrella stands with the familiar Sabrett painted in bold letters on the rim and approached the guy.

"What'll you have, miss?"

"I want a hotdog with catsup, onions, and sauerkraut, and throw in a can of Coke."

"Sure thing. That'll be four bucks."

I handed over the money, and he handed me the food. That was an even exchange. I immediately started munching the frankfurter, and it was so juicy that the liquid ran down my chin. I devoured it within about five seconds. I wiped the dribble off my face and popped open the soda. I gulped down the cold liquid, and the refreshment was immediate. I could have lived on this stuff for the rest of my life. I had heard rumors that this tasty treat contained rat and roach parts. If that was what gave it flavor, then I was all for those foreign additives in my food.

I casually walked to the train station and hopped on the F train. I got off at 7th Avenue in Brooklyn and entered the lobby of 272. In my apartment, I called Chicky. I got her voicemail and left a message. I was so excited.

I sat at my computer and began to compose another ad for Craigslist. This time, I needed to get someone to collect the creepy crawlies so I would have a visual to present to the congregated mass. My fragmented mind wandered, and I had to decide what category I would put it in. Let's see... barter, nah...household perhaps...after all, they usually party in the kitchen. Okay, I began typing: "Seeking roaches. I will pay a penny apiece. Please call Limelight ASAP at (917) 596-9850." My phone started ringing immediately after I posted it. The calls were weird. Some people wanted me to pay for a dime bag. Others were angry that I would place such an ad. I hung up on those weirdos and took another look at it. I didn't believe it was offensive. Great! Some idiot flagged the ad, and it's been removed. I was wondering why, and then it hit me. They thought that I was advertising for pot. I reworded the ad, in parentheses said, "the insect kind," and also added that I would be providing a metal, mesh cage to put them in.

I received a call from "Bill." He was excited about parting with his playmates, although he said he would miss them. "I got loads of the buggers in my walk-up studio. After the lights are turned off, they begin to party hearty," he jokingly confided. We agreed to meet at 7:00 p.m. at the Barnes and Noble in my neighborhood. I provided him with the directions on how to get there. I described my appearance to him, and he reciprocated. I grabbed the cage, which had very fine wire mesh around the sides with a pine top and bottom. The pine top had a slot which had a spring lever that I had designed especially for this purpose.

I walked over to the bookstore, and as I was crossing the street, a large SUV came barreling down and almost hit me. I gave him the finger and shrieked, "Do you think you're on the Autobahn or something, or perhaps you're just racing to your own funeral?" Upon arriving at the B&N, I ordered a coffee from Starbucks. After I paid for my drink, I took a seat. I pulled out my copy of the book *How to be a Successful Failure* and began reading on page twenty-five. I grew impatient and looked up periodically. I saw my friend Jeremy reading my favorite novel, the probing *How to Pick, Roll and Flick Your Way to Happiness*. Finally, Bill made his appearance. This guy looked like a typical hippie. He had long, wavy, greasy scraggly hair that cascaded down his slender back and a beard that looked like it already housed quite a few bugs. I reached inside my red Gucci patent leather wallet and extracted five singles and handed the cage to him as I said "Fill 'er up." I told Bill I needed it back by August 16th at 10:00 a.m. He gave me a lopsided grin, which showed me his off-white teeth, and nodded his agreement. He took the cage and got stuck in the revolving door. This guy must have smoked something funny before meeting me today. I helped him out the door and waved good-bye.

The rest of the week passed in a flurry of activity. My Uncle Sid graciously delivered my shirts on Saturday, August 7th, and as he handed them to me, I gave him the remainder of the money I owed. I then spoke to my dad about helping me since he worked for the city and could get me the permit necessary to stage this demonstration. He agreed without a second thought. I phoned Chicky and left a message about how everything was going. I thought she was avoiding me since I didn't hear back from her. Oh well, I could pull this thing off without her help or interference.

The big day finally arrived, and I called Bill and met him in front of my building. He arrived on the dot. He took the cage out of a large bag and handed it over to me.

"What the..." I asked incredulously. "These things look more like water bugs than roaches."

"Right. My cousin from Davis, California, is visiting me, and he 'borrowed' these Madagascar hissing cockroaches from his job at Bohart Museum. He gave them to me as a gift. Since they are bigger than the New York kind, I figured you would pay more money for them."

I examined these large specimens and was immediately grossed out. They were wingless yellow bugs, and they look engorged. Obviously, this guy was an idiot. Well, it was too late to exchange them for the German kind.

"I see. What is running down the cage? Is it roach juice?"

"Yeah," he sheepishly responded. "I had to stuff them in, and some of them had an early—"

"Okay." I handed him another ten bucks and shooed him away.

I raced up the stairs breathless and ran into my room with my cache. I pulled the shopping cart out but decided instead to use my Radio Flyer wagon and loaded it up with the shirts and other necessary things. I called Chicky and convinced her, with some cajoling, to accompany me, and she finally agreed.

Chicky came over and pulled the wagon to the elevator. It was almost 12 p.m. when we reached the street. We hailed a cab. The driver stopped and eyed us suspiciously. I quickly moved the black sheet I had brought to cover my moving baggage.

"Can you please help us with our stuff?" I pleadingly asked.

"Sure, no problem," he quickly responded and then said under his breath, "I hope these broads give me a big tip."

"Wow, I can't believe you speak English so well. Usually when I get a cab, I can't decipher the garbled tongue of the foreign driver."

He laughed. "There are still some natives left in the city."

I gave him my destination of the TKTS place at 47th and Broadway and then sat back and relaxed.

"Hey lady, what's the racket back there?"

"We have crickets that we're bringing to the pet store. It's a way for us to earn a little pocket money."

"Those sure don't sound like any crickets. Are you sure you don't have a snake in there?"

"Of course not. I'm deathly afraid of those things." Then I punched Chicky's leg and asked, "Isn't that so, Chicky?"

"Yes, she can't even stand to look at a picture of them."

We finally arrived, and I handed the driver a fifty and told him to "keep the change."

A big smile crept across his unshaven face.

Thanks to my kindhearted father, we had the podium and microphones already set up. The white plastic table was covered with a green cotton sheet. I shoved the box of tees underneath it. A line of people started to form immediately. After they handed me the money, Chicky asked them, "What size do you want?" then handed the shirt to them. People started putting on the tees immediately. Finally, the hour had arrived. They took their seats, and I grabbed the cage from Chicky. I was so excited that I tripped, and the cage went flying, and as it hit the ground, the wood splintered, and the roaches escaped. Pandemonium erupted as they joined the crowd. People instinctively began squashing our friends. I grabbed the microphone and reminded them to beware of roach rage. They immediately stopped the slaughter and looked up. Curious tourists joined our cause.

I adamantly declared, "We must stop the killing. Everyone here is required to search out the exterminators and steal their canisters. You can either bury them or hurl them into the sea."

The crowd erupted into cheers and shouted, "Down with Raid." After two hours, they dispersed. I noticed some children happily playing with their new friends. Chicky was horrified by this sight, but I was placated. Although this was done at first as a joke, I now felt a kinship with these cuddly companions.

After I researched the Madagascar hissing roach and learned about their eating and mating habits, I decided to go to college to become an entomologist. To help pay for college, I decided to make living brooches out of them and sell these to those who have great affection for these misunderstood creatures. They make great pets since they are docile and don't bite.

When I began this project, I had no idea that I would go from detesting these vermin to actually wanting to study these fascinating bugs. I guess I had finally found my calling in life. The money I've earned selling these brooches from roaches was enough to pay for my entomology degree. And, to this day, I continue to plead with people to "save our roaches from extinction."

Final Reprieve

As I pressed the rewind button of my mind, my jumbled thoughts came into sharp focus. It was just an ordinary Monday. I wish I could say that I had an inkling of the terrible events that were about to follow, but alas, I can't.

I love to go a wandering by the deep blue sea, and as I go, I love to sling my knapsack on my back. Valderi, Valdera, Valderi, Valdera, ha, ha, ha, Valderi, Valdera, my knapsack on my back...

"Don't touch that dial. I love this song."

"And I hate it. You listen to it every day. I'm sick of hearing it. Your hints are so obvious."

The brown plastic, imitation 1930s radio blared this familiar tune on station 96.7 FM. I looked around at the sickly green-colored paint splattered upon the walls that reminded me of vomit. Our fabric couch's fibers were filled with five years of accumulated filth. The varnish on the oval coffee table appeared to have been rubbed off by the cheap plastic place settings we always used. In the center of the living room proudly stood my husband's most cherished piece of electronics, our black-and-white television set.

"Suni, why won't you consider coming with me? We'll take the dog, and I'll make a list of everything we'll need for a comfortable stay." He shifted in his chair.

"Are you kidding me? I'm not interested in roughing it. Why don't you invite your best friend? I'm sure he'll jump at the chance to sleep in a bug-infested environment."

"Sunita, you're making this very difficult for me. Why can't we spend time together, just this once?" He sat on his red swivel chair, one arm casually draped over his thick brown hair, with a look of frustration on his handsome face.

"Well, let's see. I'm so embittered about our marital situation. Look around at this apartment and tell me what you see."

"I see a furnished place that meets my needs: you know I'm low key and don't need much to be happy." His left ankle crossed over his right ankle. His bare feet rested on his cherished, duct-taped ottoman while his right hand absently fingered his most treasured possession, an empty Budweiser beer can mobile. Gunnar lay on the matted purple 1970s shag rug. The vibe was so thick, he wagged his tail.

"Yeah, I'm well aware of your thriftiness. Or should I just say extreme cheapness. I really resent going curbside shopping for our shabby furniture.

Of course, you make it sound like an adventure. I'm sure our neighbors would be quite surprised to see their castoffs decorating our place."

I couldn't believe I sounded like such a shrew.

"Let's not get into that again. You know we have to stay on a tight budget in order to pay down our debt."

"Excuse me, you mean your debt. I never took out any student loans while attending Westlake University. I got a job and saved my money so I could afford to eat ramen noodles. You're the one who brought this debt into our marriage, and I resent it."

I couldn't control myself.

"You know, Sunita, when we were dating, you knew how stingy I was, and you still agreed to marry me. So quit your complaining. I'm tired of listening to the same song. Look, I permit you to work. How many husbands give their wives that same option?"

I heard a police siren in the background. The noise drowned out our ongoing argument for a few brief seconds. The distraction had little effect on our heated exchange of hurtful words.

"You're kidding, right? I hate my job. The only reason I work is so I can afford to buy the necessities of life, such as food and, of course, make-up. And besides, if I didn't work, we would be using the phone book pages to wipe our butts. So, don't act like I have a choice."

"Well, tough luck, baby. We're in this for the long haul. I already paid for the damn campground, and there's no refunds given. So, pack your paisley-colored bags and let's go."

"Just so you know, Jeff, I've made an appointment with a marriage therapist to work on our shambles of a marriage. I'll go on this stupid trip if you'll agree to talk to the therapist. Otherwise, take the dog. I'm sure he'll be much better company than your witch of a wife."

"Okay, it's a deal. Now start packing, and I'll meet you in the living room. Oh, and don't forget to bring your make-up. I'm sure the bears would appreciate your fake beauty."

"Keep it, you jerk, and I'll reconsider staying married to you."

After we packed for our trip, the drive proved uneventful. I looked out the window while Jeff drove with his usual stone face. Of course, our conversation was stilted. Gunnar proved to be a much better companion than my own husband. It took three long hours before we reached Monroe campsite located in beautiful Greenville, North Carolina. Other couples were milling around. It took Jeff awhile to put up the tent, and then we decided to take a leisurely walk. As we strolled hand in hand, side-by-side, we finally started talking about fixing our marriage. I really loved my husband, but I didn't feel appreciated by him. He acknowledged that his treatment of me wasn't the best, but he loved me and wanted to save our marriage.

The campgrounds were studded with flowers. It looked like a garden of gardenias. The grass glistened in the afternoon dew. It was so peaceful; the tranquility of the scene touched my angry heart and made me feel at peace with Jeff and nature. We observed some young boys jumping and splashing in the river.

"Suni, you know what's really weird? My brother almost killed me here, yet I love this place. Did I ever tell you the story of when I was a kid, my brother, Jason, tossed me into the lake and watched me flounder? I was about nine years old at the time, and I thought that I would drown since I didn't know how to swim. Well, Jason saw me splashing around and, at first, thought that I was playing a joke on him. Then I started to go underneath the water, and he dived in and saved me. We never told my parents what really happened. I really love my big brother. He's always been my source of strength. I've tried to emulate him. I never told you this, but my parents care more about one another than they did for us. They pitted us against each other. Jason was always the more accomplished one, fill in the blank. I guess I'm going to have to learn to confide in you. You're my best friend now."

"Wow, Jeff, you never opened up to me in the seven years we've been together. I'm so glad that you convinced me to come with you."

Finally, I felt like an equal in this partnership. I stood right next to him, leaning against his hard frame. I had always felt like an outsider since my husband would never confide his deepest fears with me. With his confession, it brought a kind of openness to our once closed marriage.

After that, we walked in a companionable silence. We heard the birds singing and even saw a hummingbird flying around. Jeff raced ahead of me and then chaos erupted.

"Gunnar, come back here. That stupid dog is always chasing rabbits. Dammit, Sunita, get over here now! I'm stuck in quicksand, and I can't get out."

Jeff was caught in the grips of the wet dirt. He was waist deep in the hold. The next thing I knew, the gunk reached his chest. Suddenly, this place was no longer friendly but held a touch of evil.

"Jeff, what do you want me to do? I'm scared. Help me; somebody help us! My husband is sinking!"

"Suni, calm down. Gunnar, come here, boy. Bring me that stick over here. That's a good boy. Suni, I need you to hold the other end and pull me out."

"Okay, I've got it. But, Jeff, you weigh so much more than me. How will I ever get you out?"

This task was monumental. I realized that although I truly loved Jeff, I was unable on my own to save him. It felt like a huge boulder was resting on my dainty shoulders, and it was weighing me down.

"Honey, just tug slow and easy. Please try not to panic. My life depends on your clear head. I'm sure you don't want to be a widow at such a young age."

"Jeff, stop joking at a time like this. This is serious. I don't want to lose you since we still have to work on our relationship. Gunnar, go back to the car and bark up a storm. We need reinforcements."

After what seemed like an eternity, Gunnar brought back help. Gus, another camper, was able to pull him out quickly. Tricia, Gus's wife, brought a blanket, and we covered him. I watched as his shivering shoulders began to slouch. At that moment, my once strong husband was reduced to a quivering child. Our roles had reversed. Since I was a nervous wreck, Gus took charge and drove him to the nearest hospital, Monroe General. The doctors had him stay overnight for observation. They had to check him for hypothermia. Afterwards, we drove home exhausted but alive. I gave our hero, Gunnar, a nice, juicy steak for dinner. Jeff and I slept fitfully. I guess all that excitement made us appreciate all that we had. It's been a year since that terrible episode. We went to counseling, and with hard work and determination, our relationship improved. Although we have many hard times ahead of us in this uncertain life, as long as we share the load, I think our marriage can survive.

We know you have a choice. We thank you for choosing to join one of our clubs.

Join The Fat Club; we are currently E-X-P-A-N-D-I-N-G.

Do you enjoy picking your nose? If you can pick, roll, and flick your boogers, you might be a candidate to join The Pick 'n' Flick Club.

Join our new club. We are SORE.

Save

Our

Roaches

from

Extinction

Where our motto is: They were here way before humans, and they will be here long after we are gone. Our rally will take place on Saturday, September 25, 2007, in Madison Square Garden. People for the Ethical Treatment of Roaches will be there.

Join our new Clean Joke Club. What does a banana say when you insult it? You hurt my peelings.

Join the Peter Pan I Won't Grow Up and You Can't Make Me Club. No grown-ups need apply. Milk and cookies will be served at 3 p.m. and nap time is 4 p.m. Playdates will be arranged. Mickey Mouse rules!

For couples, we now have The Men Who Shave Their Heads and The Women Who Love Them Club. We will explore the real reason men shave their heads. Is it because they are going bald? Or are they too cheap to spring for shampoo? Or can it be because it makes a handy mirror for their wives when applying lipstick?

We are now accepting applications for The Turtle Club. Are you shy? Do you blush whenever anyone talks to you? Break out of your shell! We will not meet in person for fear you might faint due to extreme introversion.

Can you keep a secret? If so, join The Secret Club. Meetings will be held at…oops I can't tell; it's a secret.

Are you one of the great unwashed? Do you have an allergy to water? Is the idea of using deodorant a foreign concept to you? Should you have been born a cat? Then The Stinky Club may be right for you.

Join us for the end of year Pity Party. Song to be played will be "Poor Poor Pitiful Me."

And, finally, for those of you who are perpetually up on your way out, please take the escalator down.

Seize the Day

Cascading condiments coasting toward caves
Antique autos acting like atrocious aardvarks
Raving rodents roasting rutabagas
Pickled petunias passing a pageant of poodles
Elderly elephants educating an elevator of elements

Deranged derelicts dabbling in drowning dachshunds
Impatient idioms ignoring iguanas
Eloping equestrians eliminating entrails
Mangled monkeys making a marvelous masterpiece

Embrace the Effervescence!

Disposable Soldiers

Let me perish from starvation's love
Open the door to the ocean's floor
Fetter my eyes so I can't decipher—
Peace is but a cold illusion—
Feed the belly of the war beast

Wrap me in a thorny blanket
Hug the bloated bellies
of ancient Greece's casualties
Goad them into poetry's pillow—
Safe and warm, oblivion speaks.

Bask in your hollow victory
Where losers abound and winners
are nowhere to be found
Cover the heart with steel pleating
Sew the metal to the skin.

Remember, death is but an island
It vomits its inhabitants
to a place that doesn't exist

Deny the anorexia of the skeleton
Where thoughts are mist
and man must die

Plead your case before a tribunal
Wearing your righteousness as
a badge of dishonor
Bathe the bloody machete
in the sea of public opinion
Watch the lies germinate in the soil of manure
Bury the defiant truth in an unmarked grave

Frozen in Time

When Death takes a holiday, where will you Be? Asleep, dreaming of loving arms enveloping you. Or perhaps running in a cornfield, the wind beckoning you back to yesteryear. Is regret creeping into your mind and causing the cobwebs to divine? That perchance you've missed the opportunity to decide on a dream that never could be. Do Not look to the past to find yourself. Otherwise, life will have been for naught. Did they not teach you that in school the Proud cannot surpass the meek? That kindness is for those who seek to help the utter fools?

MetroCard Earrings

The supplies you will need
Are easy to obtain
So that you won't go insane
They are as follows:
Used MetroCards, scissors, and tape,
Tracing paper, pen, and earwire
Jeweler's pliers, and a thick needle

The first step in making these well
Is to choose a shape you would like to sell
Use your imagination
Or let the encyclopedia be your guide

Then trace it with a pen so neat
And cut around the edges to complete

Take the shape and tape it to the MetroCard
Carefully cut around the template
The point of a needle
Will open a hole

Use pliers to open the earwire loop
Then hook the opening in the loop
Now close to finish

As you walk down the street
The swaying of the breeze
Will make your earrings dance in the wind
To the delight of the crowd gathered around
They will praise your creativity

No Time to Wait

Why is this bus always so late?
Is it so I can find a mate?
Or perhaps I can read *War and Peace*
And take my ease

My commute is no joke
Even if the bus driver is a bloke
Complaints fall on deaf ears
This results in many tears

But I need to get to class on time
Even if I have to stop on a dime
Too bad I can't walk there
It would take me at least a year

My tale is a warning to many
To save up all their pennies
And learn how to drive
So they can arrive there alive

Death Is So Filling

I saw you there with just-washed hair
A portrait of innocence
I staked you out while assuring myself
Your safety was my priority

When questioned by my oily, suave lips
Your response was very telling
For your mother forewarned you
Not to talk with strangers

You foolish child, what were you thinking
Don't you know I was a danger to your purity
Remember some of us are more sinner than saint

But first I must go to see your precious grandmother
So that I may satiate my fiendish hunger
When you arrive, you will find that
You are next on my list to devour
I hope I find that you are a tasty morsel

Stacey's Fifth Appendage

I'm sick and tired of being held against Stacey's ear. Her hands are so full of germs, and her breath smells like a toilet. I gag all the time from this. I especially hate it when she text messages her friends. I hate it when she pushes my "buttons" with those prissy French-manicured fingernails of hers. How would you like to be poked constantly? Her voice is so loud, I end up with an earache every day. And don't get me started on the way she carelessly tosses me in her "Fendi" bag full of crap. She swings her bag so much I get seasick. When she arrives home, instead of gently lowering her bag on her bed, she slams it down like a wrestler. I have the bruises to prove it.

I know all her secrets. While she gabs to her friends, I pass along the information to my other cohorts. Blackmail is so chic nowadays. Revenge against Stacey has been on my mind lately. I've been weighing the pros and cons of this. I know exactly what I'll do. I will attach my tentacles to her eardrum. She will cry to her mom, and we will be rushed to the emergency room. The intern will examine her and immediately order a CAT scan. Afterward, he will consult with a surgeon. They will discuss the options with her parents. I'm sure her folks will opt for the surgery. In my mind's eye, I see Stacey screaming hysterically, "No surgery! I love my fifth appendage so much that it has finally become a part of me."

I will rejoice when her parents insist on the surgery because it will free me from Stacey's oppression. After the decision is made, I can see how the doctors and nurses will prep for the surgery. It is a solemn occasion, as the surgeon has never seen such an extreme case as Stacey's. Stacey is wheeled into the operating room. She is given anesthesia and told to count backwards from a hundred. The doctors have already decided how they will make an incision. If they cut an artery or vein, she will bleed too much, and if they cut too far into her eardrum, she will lose her hearing. Her parents nervously pace outside the operating room. They glance continuously at the clock. The surgery lasts for about five hours.

Finally, I can imagine poor Stacey is wheeled out and placed into her room. The anesthesia wears off, and she asks her parents if the operation is a success. Her parents are overjoyed to finally have her free of the dangerous fifth appendage. Tears will slowly course down their cheeks, and they affirm the operation's success. Stacey will ask about her most prized possession: "me." Her parents will explain to her that the surgeon was so fascinated by this case that he asked if he could keep me. I now reside in an alcohol-filled jar. I am germ free and rest on top of the surgeon's desk. I will have my fifteen minutes of fame, and Stacey will be forever disconnected from me.

Just Like the Love You Have For Me

Love blossoms just like a rose, slowly
Opening its face to the sun's rays.
Then it withers and dies

And so it seems that one day
Just like your freckles in the burning sun
Youth's exuberance will slowly fade

But, alas, my sweet dew drop
I once put you up on a pedestal so high
Only to laugh when I hurled you down to the earth

A god once
Now you are mortal man
Owing to your fickle folly
Goodbye my feckless fool

Scents of My Mind

The aura of Azure by Estee Lauder
With hints of cinnamon breath
Conjured up childhood memories
Of the carefree days of youth:

Skipping, running, and leaping
Like a Jack-in-the-box they
jump out unexpectedly.

Deep within the recesses
of my mind A hand touches
the very essence of my being.

Imagine a world without a past!
This is akin to a story
without a beginning Slowly
plodding along until it finally ends.

With joy I embrace it
Fearlessly I continue riding
this chariot of life. It stops
along the way

Finally I exit to face the future.
With bated breath I wait For the
unknown to show its face

And then the memories
will ebb Back
to the recesses of my mind.

Bibliophobia

Is it wise
to revise?
To take apart
a piece of art.
To feed the masses with a word
where digestion does occur.

I hide my eyes
from a phrase.
The dictionary
is a maze.

To the making of many books
there is no ending.
Self-help, romance, mystery,
the list is mind bending.
They nourish my soul
as they boggle my senses.

Buried Alive

Where am I?
I feel like I'm suffocating
Why is it so dark in here?
Let me reach for my lighter
What the heck; these aren't my pants
Why can't I remember?

The last thing I recall
is being at a bar
Drowning my sorrows
in shots of whiskey
Man, breaking up is so hard
Why did she leave me?
I make a decent living
Zoe, get me out of here

Falling down and blacking out
Acute alcohol poisoning
Right, the paramedic exclaimed
The ambulance rushes past
My vitals are nonexistent

Am I really dead
or just sleeping
I bang on the splintered lid
Knocking, let me out
No sound emerges

I feel something crawling
all over my face
I scream but no words form
The nightmare has begun

Before contemplating marriage, you must meet your perspective mate. After dating for a while, observing your beloved's qualities, foibles—minor character faults, you get engaged. Then the preparation for marriage begins. If you are smart, you and your honey will go for premarital counseling. You both want to be sure about this major life-altering/changing decision, because you know that once you say I do, there is no turning back, no possibility of an annulment, separation, or divorce. Marriage is a lifelong commitment involving loyalty and love. Remember that you're also marrying his/her family members. Therefore, you must learn to compromise. This illustration means the agreement you make with Tessa is the airtight marriage contract. The family is the team members. The actual marriage is Hollywood—the big guys.

When wedding anniversaries are celebrated, the first gift is usually paper. But if we stay married for sixty years, we will be rewarded with a diamond. This precious gem will last forever.

When you're traveling on the train, you don't get off before your stop. You continue on your journey until you reach your destination.

When climbing the mountain, you have a rope tied securely around your stomach, and this rope is attached to your climbing buddy/teammate. As your teammate ascends—moves upward—you are being propelled with him or her. If you choose to take out your knife and cut your rope, you are, in essence, committing suicide. Thus, when you are working on a project and change your mind—have doubts—about the success of said project and excuses easily escape your lips, you are committing professional suicide. You are, in effect, preventing yourself from achieving your goal by putting a stumbling block in your path.

WEDDING ANNIVERSARIES
First Paper
Second Cotton
Third Leather
Fourth Books
Fifth Wood or Clocks
Sixth Iron
Seventh Copper, Bronze, or Brass
Eighth Electrical Appliances
Ninth Pottery
Tenth Tin, Aluminum
Eleventh Steel
Twelfth Silk or Linen
Thirteenth Lace

Fourteenth Ivory
Fifteenth Crystal
Twentieth China
Twenty-Fifth Silver
Thirtieth Pearl
Thirty-Fifth Coral, Jade
Fortieth Ruby
Forty-Fifth Sapphire
Fiftieth Gold
Fifty-Fifth Emerald
Sixtieth Diamond

Dare to be different. These words are branded on my brain. Be a positive Polly, not a negative Nelly. Don't be your own personal stumbling block, but instead become the cheerleader to your success. Live your dreams. Make it happen. Just do it. This fat, fabulous female wants to own a house. If every person who watches this sends one dollar to PayPal on my behalf to makemewealthy@yahoo.com, I will become the proud owner of said house. I will pack my bags, write some prose, and promise to provide happiness to other people. I will randomly pick one person to receive an appreciation gift of a pair of MetroCard earrings, a Metro slinky, and a Metro wallet. All of these items are handmade by me. Please have all pets, children, or overly sensitive folks out of the room when listening to my fingernails on a chalkboard rendition of my original song entitled "Thunder Thighs."

They call me thunder thighs
Well, baby, I can't lose my mind
Cause they say it again and again
With my thunder
Oooh, my thunder thighs

They call me wide ride
Well, baby, I don't know why
Cause they say it again and again
With my wide
Oooh, my wide ride

Chorus
Jiggle your jello, mushy, cushy, tushy; flap your turkey arms, abs of flab, buns of blubber; can you pinch more than an inch, love handles, saddlebags.

One Cat Whisker

"One Cat Whisker" was left on my pillow by my daughter's cat Shugga. This small keepsake represents the love the cat has for me. This reminds me of the chocolates you find on your pillow when you stay in an expensive hotel. The whisker measures three inches from tip to root. It is as flexible as a toothbrush filament. It has a smooth surface. It is white with twelve inches of black. The black root is thick, and it gradually tapers out at the end, which becomes white. The whiskers are attached to nerves in the skin and act as delicate sense organs. Cat whiskers are composed mainly of keratin, a tough fibrous protein substance forming the outer layer of epidermal structures such as hair, nails, or horns.

Where in the world is Avi Colon? (Brooklyn)

My boss, the infamous Avi Colon, is hidden away somewhere in Brooklyn, or perhaps he is hanging out with his friends in Washington Square Park blissfully unaware that me and his mama are worrying ourselves to death.

His phone is temporarily not in service.

Has he been kidnapped by his many amorous female fans? Or have the fumes of his Aramis cologne engulfed him in flames? Or perhaps he is engrossed in reading the latest *Where's Waldo* book.

I want the best detective to find this babe magnet immediately.

Location: New York

http://newyork.craigslist.org/brk/laf/1125714525.html

One comment for "Where in the world is Avi Colon? (Brooklyn)"

1. Wow I feel like a celebrity since you published my ad on your website. Do you actually know the famous Avi Colon? I certainly didn't when I first met him.

All State Investigations
P.O. Box 7589
501 Stillwells Corner Rd., Suite A-2
Freehold, NJ 07728

June 6, 2009

Dear Miss Smith

    This letter is pursuant to our phone conversation on April 15, 2009, concerning a Mr. Avi Colon. I have done some further research on this person and have concluded that his real name is Gustave Delgado. He is originally from Santiago, Chile, and according to my sources in Scotland Yard is the famous diamond thief. Inspector McNabb has been trying to catch this thief for fifteen years. Gustave is very slippery, no doubt he drenches himself in olive oil instead of putting it on his salad. Anyway, he has a number of cohorts that he connects with in every city. The woman named Sarah Rice-A-Roni is actually a fabrication—she doesn't exist. Kevin, the Irish red-headed thirty-five-year-old, is part of his organization, the second in command. Gustave has been featured on *America's Most Wanted* and was on the FBI's most-wanted list for the past ten years. This man is dangerous. He uses a black stallion to commit these crimes. Also, after listening to the CD of his voice, I now know why he calls his band Avi and the Wolves. He sounds like a hyena in heat. And the fake woman's voice in the background, thanks to the advanced sound technology available today, is so patently ridiculous. He travels the world with a gypsy woman named Sarina. This is his common-law wife. They have about twenty-five kids; she gets pregnant every year. Apparently she's very fertile, and he's known as the greatest lover in the world. He lures lonely, unsuspecting, gullible green-eyed women with his missing teeth and goofy grin to his lair. After stripping them of their money and valuables, he dumps them in a dead-end street with his guitar as a trophy. This man is dangerous, and you should avoid him at all costs. A tracking device has been implanted in his Washburn guitar. We know his every move. The changing of his shirts represents the changing personalities he is able to put on effortlessly. Remember, Miss Smith, if he is attractive to women, then he is also attractive to men. He does not want a good wife. His intentions toward you are not honorable. By the way, after perusing the photo you sent me of yourself, I have decided to ask you to marry me. I am well known in the internet world as a chubby chaser, and I love green eyes, so please give me a call at 1-800-94-TRUTH. If you will take me up on my offer, I will waive the fee for our investigation work. Thank you for allowing my company to investigate this scoundrel.

Sincerely,
Justin Case

Joseph,

I'm writing you this letter in the hope that you'll reconsider cutting your nubs. Here are a few reasons not to cut them:
1. Nubs have feelings too.
2. Nubs are sensitive to pain. You will have to live with their screams until your hair grows back in.
3. People will call you stubby.
4. This dinosaur has nubs—see how happy he is. After they were removed, dinosaurs became extinct.

Please visit our new website at WWW.SAVEOURNUBS.COM.

An informal survey was conducted over the internet. Three million people voted to keep the nubs; two voted to cut them off. We here at SON believe you voted twice.

Gustave Alexander Delgado is a worldly man. He is a lover of women and a very romantic man. He lives by the code of the caballeros. Elena Rosita is a virgin. She is twenty-one years old and has been pledged to Senor Delgado. She is extremely close to her father.

External: Washington Square Park

Gustave

(Seated on park bench.) Miss, why are you crying? You're much too pretty to let sadness mar your face. (Hands her his handkerchief.)

Elena

I just found out from my father that he has promised me in marriage to his best friend. I'm scared and don't want to marry this ogre.

Gustave

Come closer. (He gently takes her hand and rests it in his cupping it.) Perhaps if you confide in someone, it won't seem so scary. Do you have a friend or relative that you trust with your feelings?

Elena

No, actually my best friend is my father. I'm so distraught. I thought he loved me, yet he's forcing me into this disastrous union. I love my freedom, and a husband will hinder it.

Gustave

Maybe. But you'll enjoy an intimate, loving relationship, namely sex. Did you know that a good sex life helps you live longer? I just read that little tidbit in *Esquire*.

Elena

Sir, what you're saying is shocking to me. I never discuss such private matters with anyone, not even my dad. (Her cheeks turn ten shades of red.)

Gustave

Come now. You're a grown woman. It's a natural part of life. I enjoy a good roll in the hay from time to time. But if it offends your sensibilities, I will cease this foolish talk. Let me formally introduce myself, I'm Alex, and you are?

Elena

Leaving. I usually don't talk to strangers. (She gets up and walks toward the Garibaldi fountain. He follows her.)

Gustave

Wait. Can we at least exchange phone numbers? Perhaps I can speak to your father. He might reconsider.

Elena

Oh no, I could never bring a strange man into our house. Once my dad, Pietro, makes up his mind, he won't change it. It's the curse of the Geneva clan of Tuscany.

Gustave

Well, if you're sure. Can I at least buy you coffee? There's a neat little java joint called Leaf and Bean. We can chat.

Elena

Um, okay. (They slowly stroll to the store.)

Cashier

Hello, what would you like to order?

Gustave

Let's see. I'll have the large organic French roast, a piece of cherry pie, and… (points to companion.)

Elena

A small hazelnut and death by chocolate brownie, please.

Cashier

That'll be twenty dollars.

Gustave

(Hands her the money.) Thanks, sweetheart. (They sit outside and chat while wolfing down the goodies.)

Elena

(Looks at watch.) Wow, it's already six. I've got to get home and make dinner for Dad. Thanks for the meal. Bye.

Gustave

Can I see you again?

Elena

I'm not sure. My wedding is in one month, and I've got to begin preparing for it.

Gustave

Hey, what if I help you? I've got a good eye for fashion. And you did tell me you don't have a best friend to talk to. What'd you say?

Elena

Well, okay. I guess it can't hurt. And I do need a man's opinion on what guys like.

Gustave

Great. See you tomorrow, same time, same channel.

Elena

Sure. (They shake hands.) And by the way, my name's Rosita, but everyone calls me Rosie.

Gustave

Hi Rosie, ready to plan your funeral?

Elena

(Laughs.) Well, that's one way of putting it. I've become resigned to my fate. Marrying a man my fathers' age is disgusting. But I trust that my dad won't fix me up with a cruel man. I made a list of all the places I need to go. First, I want to register with Bergdorf Goodman. I'm sure our rich guests won't have a problem paying for our gifts.

Gustave

I can tell that you're such a kind person. (He says sarcastically.) No one would object.

Elena

Okay, shall we go? (She playfully hooks her arm through his and they stroll away. They register at BG and then go to pick out her dress at Vera Wang's.)

Salesgirl

Can I help you?

Elena

Yes, I'm here to pick out my wedding gown. I take a size six.

Salesgirl

Do you know what kind of style you'd be interested in? Do you like a particular fabric? Silk is all the rage now.

Elena

I love lace brocade. Off white with seed pearls. I would wear my mother's dress, but she was smaller than me.

Salesgirl

Come with me. (Shows her the rack while Gus checks out the quality of the fabric.) The dressing rooms are right over there. If you need more help, please call me. My name is Christina.

Elena

Thanks, Christina, for your help. (She tries on various dresses and twirls around to the bemusement of Gus.)

Gustave

You remind me of a prima ballerina. I think this dress is perfect. It shows off your best asset.

Elena

You mean my boobs?

Gustave

No. (He laughs.) Your lovely green eyes. But your boobs are nice too.

Elena

Stop. (She blushes, then pulls up her long wavy hair.) I want my hair in ringlets. After watching *Gone with the Wind*, I know I'll look cute.

Gustave

(He gently moves her hands away, and her hair spreads out.) Your hair is so soft. I want to twirl it around my fingers. I want to see it spread out on your pillow. (A sly smile escapes his lips.)

Elena

(She abruptly pulls away.) Please don't talk like that. My future husband wouldn't approve.

Gustave

Sorry. (Looks contrite.) But your beauty overwhelmed me for a moment. Henceforth (pledges) I'll always conduct myself in your presence like the gentleman I am. Please excuse my barbaric behavior. (He gallantly bows.)

Elena

(Confusion crosses her face.) Sure, whatever. So, you think I should purchase this dress? (He nods. She turns to Christina.) I'll take the dress. Please charge it to my American Express card.

Salesgirl

Okay. Would you like this delivered, or will you pick it up later?

Elena

Please deliver it to this address. (Scribbles address on pad.) (As they walk, Gus suggests they feed the pigeons. He hands her a bag of breadcrumbs.) How sweet. What made you think of this?

Gustave

As a hobby, I like to read people's body language. I can see you love animals. Shall we? (They take a seat on the bench and silently toss bread to the eager birds.)

Elena

(Looks at her watch.) I gotta go. What's on our list for tomorrow?

Gustave

Ah, yes, the infamous list. We could call the caterers. Do you have a guest list written yet? I could help you compose one.

Elena

Actually, no. I will invite all my father's friends. Plus, my cousin, Natasha. I'm sure she'll snicker when she finds out I'm marrying an old man. She's always been jealous of me. I'll endure her barbs, calmly. (She laughs.)

Gustave

Your laugh is like a gentle wave. It pushes sad thoughts into the background. I'll walk you home.

Elena

Thanks, but I don't want my dad to see me with another man. See ya tomorrow. (She runs like the breeze.)

Elena

Hey, Alex, why so glum?

Gustave

I was just thinking that I'd miss your company once you're married.

Elena

I'm sure my new husband wouldn't approve of my male friends. I wonder if he's the jealous type.

Gustave

So then, you've never met him.

Elena

When I was little, I remember him visiting, but that was ages ago. I wouldn't recognize him if he plopped himself down next to me.

Gustave

Good. I've heard that Dean and DeLuca is a great place to eat. Care to join me?

Elena

Sure, but only if you let me pay for myself. My dad gives me a generous allowance. (They take the R train to Prince Street.) Everything looks so delicious. Look at the cakes. One has small candy bees on top. I wonder if they make wedding cakes.

Gustave

I know a place that specializes in delicious cakes. After we eat, can we go there? Everything is custom made.

Elena

That sounds great.

Cashier

That'll be twenty dollars please.

Elena

(They walk until they reach Ferrara Bakery. Elena's eyes get wide. She looks like a curious child. They enter the store and breathe in the aroma of flavors) I love coconut. I wanna get a coconut cake with cherry filling and chocolate buttercream frosting.

Gustave

That sounds like an interesting combination. Did you just make that up, or have you tried it before?

Elena

No, but I'm known in my household as the creative cook. I make up all my own recipes. I've even written a cookbook, although I haven't gotten it published yet. Procrastination is my middle name. (Looks pensive.)

Gustave

You're a very talented young lady. I'm sure your new hubby will put on the required fifteen pounds of weight within the first year of married life.

Elena

I hope not. I don't want to be married to a penguin.

Cashier

We'll need a 50 percent deposit on this order.

Elena

Sure, no problem. Do you take checks?

Cashier

Yes, with a valid form of ID.

Elena

Great. Who do I make the check out to?

Cashier

Ferrara Bakery.

Elena

(Hands check to cashier. Turns to Gus.) Where to now?

Gustave

I'm beat. Let's go eat. There's a nice Thai restaurant down the street. My treat.

Elena

(Smiles.) How sweet. Okay, my feet hurt. I've got to stop wearing high heels. (Arm in arm.) (After eating, they head home to their respective residences.)

Gustave

(Rain blanketed the city. They head for the nearest Starbucks located at Astor Place.) Hi honey, what's on your list of things to do today?

Elena

Just relax. I've made all the arrangements. Actually, I do have my list right here. (Pulls out list and pen and begins checking off.) Rented hall—check, catering—check, cake—check, dress—check, groom? (He glances over her shoulder with a puzzled look.)

Gustave

Why did you put a question mark next to groom? Are you having second thoughts?

Elena

No, but maybe he is. I've never even seen this man. He doesn't call me. It's really weird.

Gustave

He's just nervous. No man wants to be roped and leg shackled to just one woman. We like variety. I fondly recall the time...

Elena

Spare me the details if it involves you, a woman, and a bed.

Gustave

Jealous, are you? Have you already fallen at the feet of the greatest lover in history?

Elena

Don Juan?

Gustave

No, silly, I meant me.

Elena

Hardly. Can we please change the subject? You're embarrassing me,

Gustave

I wouldn't want those virginal ears of yours to be exposed to such shocking things. Didn't your father ever speak to you about the facts of life?

Elena

No. My mother died when I was twelve. He's kind of a Victorian guy. We never discuss those things.

Gustave

Okay, it you're uncomfortable about it, I'll stop. Your wedding night will be when all the gory details are revealed.

Elena

Right, okay, where shall we go?

Gustave

How about Central Park? I haven't been there in years. And I have some cracked corn to feed the ducks.

Elena

How sweet of you. Okay, let's go. (Central Park.) This is so much fun. It's so peaceful. I want to see if they will eat right out of my hand. Look, they're waddling toward me, and the baby duckling is pecking the corn.

Gustave

Ah hah, even the ducks love you. Let's eat. I brought some food for us. (Takes his backpack off and shows her the contents.) I've got port wine cheese, water crackers, and some roast beef sandwiches on baguette and a bottle of champagne. We can sit on the grass. I even brought a blanket.

Stranger

Gus, is that you? Man, I haven't seen you in at least ten years. Still hawking real estate? (They embrace.)

Gustave

Bob, wow, what have you been up to? Yes, and I'm making a killing. I own the Manse on 8th Street.

Stranger

Who's the little filly by your side? You've always been a babe magnet. I remember your mantra: I knew 'em before I screw 'em. Funny, huh?

Gustave

This is my friend, Rosie. (They shake hands.) We were just about to have some lunch. Care to join us?

Stranger

I'd love to, but I got a power lunch to go to. Let's exchange numbers, and we can arrange a meeting. I'm in the market for a condo. (They trade business cards.) Listen, Gus. I never told you this, but when my wife died, you were the only friend I had. I owe you big time. Ask of me anything, and it's yours. (They embrace.) Bye.

Elena

Your friend called you Gus. Do you mind explaining this discrepancy to me? (Arms across her chest, toe tapping.)

Gustave

That's my first name, short for Gustave. Alex is my middle name. I go by both names.

Elena

Please don't tell me your last name is Delgado. (Distress clearly written on her tortured face.)

Gustave

Actually, yes, I'm your husband to be. Can we discuss this rationally? We could partake of the food I brought and calmly talk this over.

Elena

Really, do I look stupid to you? You've purposely hidden your true identity from me. You deceived me; why? You knew who I was that first time, didn't you? You planned this charade; why? Do you despise me? Were you trying to spy on me? Speak, you fool!

Gustave

Okay. (Puts his hands up.) You win. I did. I've wanted you since that time I glimpsed you walking in the garden. I was talking to your father, just gazing out the window, and I saw you feeding the birds. You had the most beneficent, serene smile I'd ever seen. In that moment, I had to possess you.

Elena

You lied to me! I trusted you!

Gustave

I thought that if I were allowed to properly court you, you wouldn't resent this forced marriage. (Goes to hug her.)

Elena

Don't (pause) touch (pause) me! You bastard. You're an idiot. I'm not a thing to possess, but a woman who needs the love of a kind man. I hate you! (She moves to storm away, but he quickly embraces her while she's alternately crying and screaming and pummeling him with her closed fists.) Let (pause) me (pause) go, you brute. (She sobs.)

Gustave

I'll release you as soon as you promise not to run from me. (She nods yes. He slowly releases his hold on her.)

Elena

(She kicks him on the shin.) Jerk. (She marches away.)

Gustave

Hey, what did you do that for? You little minx. You promised not to run away.

Elena

I kept my promise. (Head turns back to him.) Technically, I'm not running but stomping away.

Gustave

(He follows closely behind her.) Rosie, please come back. I don't want you mad at me. We're friends, remember?

Elena

You're dense. I'm not your friend. Don't worry, I'll still show up for our sham wedding. My job now is to make your life so miserable that you'll file for divorce ASAP.

Gustave

Don't bet on it. Once that ring is on your dainty little finger, it stays until death do us part. (Laughs.)

Elena

You're a cruel man. (Tears coursing down her cheek.)

Pietro

My darling daughter, look at you. You're the most beautiful bride, next to your mother, that is. Why the tears?

Elena

Oh Father, Gus is a terrible person. He tricked me.

Pietro

I thought you never met the man. (Hugs her.) Tell me about it.

Elena

Well, that day that you ambushed me with the news of my upcoming wedding to this virtual stranger. I was so distraught that I went to the park to weigh my options. I've never disobeyed you before, but well, this was a shock.

Pietro

How did you find out?

Elena

Well, he spoke to me, and we became fast friends, although I do find him crude at times. Anyway, he volunteered to come with me to all the places to prepare for this day. Last week, while we were in Central Park, his friend called his name, and it's a mess.

Pietro

I'm missing some information here. I thought you said you were friends with him,

Elena

Yes, but he told me his name was Alex. If I knew he was my future husband, I wouldn't have consorted with the enemy. (Still crying.)

Pietro

(Leads her to the couch, and they take a seat. He places her hands in his.) I've known Gus for years. I always thought it strange that he never married. I was sure he was a confirmed bachelor. But all that changed when he saw you. He reacted like a dog in heat. I know he has a reputation as a player, but now he's ready to settle down. Gus is a wealthy man, and you won't want for anything.

Elena

(Said in a whisper.) Except love, perhaps.

Pietro

Come, my love, dry those tears. We have to get you ready to meet your future. Everything will work out. I promise. (Gently guides her upstairs.)

Elena

Thank you, Father. You've always been the one steady thing in my life. I'll always love you.

Reverend

Do you, Gustave Alexander Delgado, take Elena Rosita Geneva to be your wedded wife? To have and to hold, from this day forward, for better for worse, for richer for poorer, in sickness or in health, to love and to cherish, till death do us part. And hereto I pledge you my faithfulness.

Gustave

I do.

Reverend

Do you, Elena Rosita Geneva, take Gustave Alexander Delgado to by your wedded husband? To have and to hold, from this day forward, for better for worse, for richer for poorer, in sickness or in health, to love and to cherish, till death do us part. And hereto I pledge you my faithfulness.

Elena

Can I think about that for a minute, or better yet, can I poll the audience? What say you? Should I marry this specimen of deception? This elderly gentleman, a deflowerer of innocent virgins? Speak up.

Heckler

Marry the stud already, so we can eat.

Elena

Well, it's unanimous. Yes.

Reverend

I now pronounce you husband and wife. You may kiss the bride.

Gustave

With pleasure. (Whispers in her ear.) No chaste kiss. I want one filled with passion like this. (It's filled with anger, passion, and a touch of revenge. When the kiss ends.) You will crave my kisses, my touch. I will brand you for eternity; you are mine! (He suddenly releases his grip, and she stumbles only to be rescued by Gus. He puts his arm through hers, and they walk over to the guests.) Smile, darling, I wouldn't want our guests to see you unhappy. (They mingle with the guests.)

Gustave

(Back home in the bedroom.) Wow, I'm bushed. I'm sorry we're not taking our honeymoon just yet, but my work beckons. I'm going to be extremely gentle with you since this is your first time. Come over here.

Elena

(Nervous and begins rambling.) Shouldn't we change first? I mean, I want to get out of my dress. I could put on my nightgown or perhaps a long T-shirt.

Gustave

What would be the point of that? I'm just going to remove every stitch of clothing. Don't be scared. I promise, if it's too painful, I'll finish quickly, okay. Come here and let me unzip your dress. (She permits him to do this. As he slowly performs this task, he massages her shoulders.) Relax. (He whispers into her ear.) The best is yet to come. (The dress slips to the floor.) He gazes at her near naked body. She flees to the bed and covers herself with the blanket. He walks over to her and looks down. Then kneels and strokes her hair.) Rosie, darling, please don't make this difficult. Afterwards, if you wish for me to sleep in another room, I will. Okay, honey? (She nods her head.)

Elena

Alex, please don't tell me step by step what you're going to do; just do it and get it over with.

Gustave

Sure, princess. Okay, let's do it. (She removes her bra and panties. Tears slip down her cheeks. He speeds it up and finishes inside her.) I'll see you in the morning. (Says this dismissively.) Why don't you take a nice bubble bath. It'll lessen the pain.

Elena

Thanks for your concern. (She says this sarcastically.) What, you don't want to have another go? Please just leave.

Gustave

Contrary to what you might think, I care about you deeply and would be very upset if I found you missing. (He puts on his robe and kisses the top of her head.) Sweet dreams.

Gustave

(Sitting at dining room table reading his newspaper.) Rosie, what would you like to eat? My talented chef, Hans, made an assorted array of the most delicious food. (He moves his hand across the table for emphasis.) I'm sure there's something here tempting for your tummy. How about a Southwest omelet with buttered toast and bacon? We have some yummy coffee. A glass of fresh squeezed orange juice would perk you up.

Elena

Stop treating me like a child! You will now address me as Elena.

Gustave

Listen, my dear, I'm calling you Rose from now on, because you're a blossoming flower whose scent is sweet and heady to my nose.

Elena

Screw you.

Gustave

It's more enjoyable with you, my love.

Elena

(She tosses the contents of her glass at his face and runs away to their bedroom where she locks the door and then flings herself on the bed sobbing.) I hate him.

Gustave

(He sits there stunned for about two minutes, wipes his face, and goes to take a shower and change his sticky clothes.)

Gustave

(Later that evening, about 7 p.m.) Rose, can I please talk to you in my study? It's important.

Elena

Of course, Alex

Gustave

I don't appreciate getting soaked in juice. From now on, you will refrain from such antics. I will not tolerate disrespect from my mate, understood?

Elena

Listen, darling. I'm not one of your robotic servants you can push around. Don't command, ask. (She walks away and goes to the door to leave.)

Gustave

Wait. (Strides over to her and quickly handcuffs her to him.) Now we are going to sit and discuss our marriage.

Elena

(Shock etches her face. She meekly follows him to the couch.) Please take the jewelry off my wrist. I hate being confined.

Gustave

Shut up and listen. I won you in a poker game with your dad. He's a great player when sober, but when drunk, I'm better.

Elena

Liar! My father would never gamble with my future. Anyway, he rarely drinks. You tricked him, didn't you?

Gustave

Not exactly. We always have a friendly game of poker every Wednesday. After he consumed a good amount of brandy, I just suggested off handedly that he bet your hand in marriage. The rest, as they say, is history.

Elena

(She sobs.) I don't believe it. My father would never betray his only child.

Gustave

Okay, let's see him now. He won't lie to you. (Unlocks handcuffs.)

Pietro

Hello, Rosie (Gives her a big hug.) Hi Gus. How's married life?

Gustave

I'm adjusting well. It's wonderful having a warm body next to me every night. But it's taking your daughter longer to get use to it. Will you please tell Rose how we came to be in this predicament?

Pietro

You mean the arrangement.

Gustave

Yes.

Pietro

(Turns to his daughter with sheepish grin.) I lost you in a poker game. I usually don't imbibe much, but well, you know, Gus is very persuasive and kept refilling my glass with that delicious cherry brandy, and I, uh, well, you know, one thing led to another, and here we all are.

Elena

(Tears filling her empty eyes.) No, Papa, how could you do such a terrible thing? Is it because of money? I would have been happy to get a job.

Pietro

No, child. I was worried. You seemed so content staying with me, but one day I won't be here, and I wanted you to experience the same kind of loving marriage your mom and me had. I didn't want you to end up a spinster.

Elena

You could've told me. I was happy being free. A controlling husband was the last thing I wanted. Now my life is over.

Pietro

Come now, Gus is a good man.

Elena

(Jumps up.) Father, you are dead to me. How could you betray me like this? (Runs out.)

Gustave

She's a lot of trouble.

Pietro

Give her time, Gus. She needs to digest this information. I know my daughter; she'll eventually come to grips with this. Let's have a drink; you'll need to fortify yourself against that stubborn gal.

Gustave

Sure, I'm thirsty. (Gets drunk.)

Gustave

(Enters bedroom at 3:00 a.m. and slips into bed) Okay, honey, time to do your wifely duty. I'm up for some loving.

Elena

Don't ever approach me drunk. I want you to remember the pleasure sober. Besides, I'm sure you can't perform in the state you're in.

Gustave

You're so wrong. I could be blasted, but my friend here is always at attention.

Elena

You're so crude. Please just sleep it off. Tomorrow's another day.

Gustave

No bitch turns me down. I'm not averse to forcing you. Don't push my buttons.

Elena

You've proclaimed that you're a gentleman. Do you want me to have more reasons to hate you?

Gustave

I don't care anymore. (He advances on her and overpowers her. Rips her nightgown. He pushes his knee between her legs, takes his hand and makes sure she's slick, and then slides his member into her. She stops struggling and submits to him. Afterwards, he starts snoring.)

Gustave

(It's 8:00 a.m.) Hey, honey. (Kisses her.) I'm taking the day off from work. Let's go do something. We could go see a movie, or perhaps, you have some fondness for wildlife, we could go to the Bronx Zoo. I haven't been there since I was a kid.

Elena

You must be joking. Last night you raped me, and today you act like everything is normal between us.

Gustave

What are you talking about? I remember coming home, and then I blacked out.

Elena

(She holds up her torn nightgown.) This is what you did to me last night.

Gustave

No, God, no. I'm so sorry. I've never in my life forced myself upon any woman. I must have been out of my mind with anger. Please forgive me.

Elena

Don't bother apologizing. Just go.

Java Junkie

Darla came running into the house like a tornado chasing a storm, the screen door slamming shut with a resounding bang. "What in tarnation is that loud noise? Darla Marie Baker, how many times have I told you not to slam that dang door."

"Sorry, Ma." She held a piece of paper clenched tightly up in her fist. "Mama, mama, I got a letter from Charla," Darla breathlessly declared, "and she said I could be her roommate in NYC."

Bertha grabbed it out of her hand and scanned it. After perusing it, she threw it on the floor. "Honey, why would you want to leave Normal, Alabama, to live in Sin City? That place is full of folks who pierce their skin and get tattoos on parts of their body that are just too indecent to mention. They drink designer coffee and hard liquor, and they got no manners. Them city folk are controlled by the devil hisself. Just yesterday I spoke to Pastor Shepherd, and he expounded upon them godless New Yorkers. He told me they are all atheists. They got no soul. Plus, that Charla is a loosey goosey."

"Mama, Charla has lived in Manhattan for two long years, and ain't nobody mugged or molested her. Although her apartment is considered small, according to Charla, 'it is no larger than a barn,'; she's made it comfy. Besides, I'm eighteen now, just finished high school, was a straight-A student who never caused you and Pa any trouble."

"Honey, you're right, but hear me out. The people in New York City are cold and rude, just like the weather there. They lack compassion like the people in Alabama.

"Do you remember your great Aunt Beulah? She owned a diner on Marietta Way, and that woman showed hospitality to friends and strangers alike. When people couldn't pay their bill, she always told them, 'Pay when you can, t'aint no rush.' The town drunk would wait at the back of the diner for her to toss away food scraps. Beulah would invite him into the diner and feed him a hot meal. She made mounds of garlic mashed potatoes, and her herb-fried chicken was the talk of the town. No one could duplicate her peach pie crumble. She dealt with that lazy, no-good husband of hers, Bubba, with such patience and kindness. Do you think the good people of New York would feed a hungry person? Hell no! They'd just let him starve on the cement pavement.

"Darla, ask your pa what he thinks about these plans of yers. As soon as you leave these here parts, yer gonna change and become high fallutin'. Y'all forget all about us."

"Ma, you know that ain't so; you and Pa is all I've got. I just want the freedom to pursue my dreams. I want to go to school and become a beautician. I know I have the talent since I've been cutting you and Pa's hair since I was thirteen."

"Darla, come and sit with me on the couch. There's something I've been a meaning to tell you for years. It's a secret me and yer pa have been wrestling with. When I was pregnant, I was expecting doubles. At the times, I didna know 'cause we didna have enough money for a sonogram. When it was time for you to be born, I was insane with worry. My water broke at 3 a.m., and your pa rushed me to the hospital. We arrived at Community General just in time. The doctors and nurses put me in a wheelchair and took me inta the delivery room. I was a screaming them curses and just carrying on like a banshee until they got the first baby out. A hush fell over the room, and the Dr. Johnson solemnly explained to me the baby was stillborn. For nine months, I carried a dead youngun in me. The nurse gingerly handed the bundled baby to me. She was a real beauty. Full head of shiny black hair and skin so pale and translucent you could see her tiny capillaries. I was bawling my eyes out. Then the doctor said he saw another head. I pushed and out you flew. Yer daddy done caught you just like a football. You were placed in my other arm. I named you Darla on the spot. Yer daddy then took you and held you close and made a promise to you that he would protect you and never let anyone ever hurt you. Then he gently brushed his mustache across your crimson cheeks.

"Three days later, we left the hospital with you all bundled up against the chilly December weather. That same day we attended the funeral of your twin, Dream. I named her that because she was a dream, never really real to us since we never saw her take a breath.

"Every year on your birthday, December 5, we always visit her grave at Temple Cemetery. Me and yer pa always leave lilac flowers on her grave because her eyes were the color of lavender." Taking Darla's hands, Bertha looked into her daughter's eyes with unshed tears and asked her if she wanted to visit Dream's grave.

"Yes, Mama, since now I understand why you were so overprotective toward me when I was growing up."

Exactly one year later, on an overcast January day in 2001, Darla showed up at her parents' home. She banged on the screen door and started yelling their names. After opening up the door, her mom took one look at her disheveled appearance, which included torn and filthy clothing, bloodshot eyes, matted hair, and the shakes, that Bertha almost fainted. This person looked nothing like her precious Darla. After the initial shock wore off, she invited Darla into the warm house, took her into the kitchen, and made her favorite drink, a hot cup of chocolate with mini marshmallows, and asked her what happened. When Darla began her story, her dad excused himself from their presence and went into his bedroom. He wondered what hard drugs she was on and was determined to get her the help she needed to break free from this ugly addiction.

As Darla breathed in the rich scent of chocolate, she began to open up to her mother. "After I said my good-byes to you and Pa, I boarded the Greyhound bus. I sat in the back by the window next to this real pretty old lady. I come ter find out her name was Verna Marlow, and she had the biggest, puffiest ball of white hair that she kept on the top of her head, held together with about a zillion bobby pins. She wore a brocaded blue dress that reminded me of *Gone with The Wind*. That there dress smelled so musty, I thought it must have been about a hundred years old. She told me she was eighty-four years old and her grandkids lived in New York and she was a going there to take care of them for a couple of years. This woman here about chewed my ear off. I tried mighty hard to ignore her. I broke out the magazines you gave me and started reading *Country Living*, but she kept on her a yammering. Then I decided to pretend to sleep. But that didn't put her off, so finally, I pulled out the earplugs you gave me and stuck them in my ears and just drifted off to sleep. The next thing I knew, we was in New York City. The driver told us to take all our belongings with us.

"Charla met me at Penn Station and helped me with my luggage. She gave me the biggest hug. We had lunch at Au Bon Pain. I ordered the Arizona chicken sandwich with a soda pop. It was so good, and then she took me to her apartment. She lives in Hell's Kitchen. We took the train there, and while we were riding, I told her that my mother warned me about the Devil's lair, and here I was, smack dab in the middle of Hell. Charla's apartment was so beautiful. She told me she furnished it with the cast-offs of her neighbors. She showed me around town, and the streets were so dirty, a trail of black gum littered the streets. The people never smiled, and when I shouted out "Howdy," they averted their eyes from me. Darla pulled me aside and explained to me that in New York the people were afraid of getting mugged, so they never said hello. After that, I acted like I was a native New Yorker. After walking for about three hours I was all tuckered out, so we headed to a Chinese restaurant, aptly named the Lotus

Flower, and chowed down on shrimp lo mein until we were full. Then we went home. I slept on her Ikea paisley sofa.

"The next morning, Charla woke me up at 6 a.m. and told me I needed to look for a job. I told her I didn't have any skills, so she encouraged me to apply for a job at Starbucks as a barista. I bought a weekly, unlimited MetroCard and headed to the Astor Street location. The manager, Mr. Cornell, was very kind. He gave me an application, and I filled it out and handed him my resume. He looked it over and asked me if I was available for overtime. I told him no problem. He said that he was interviewing other people but would get back to me in about a week. I then went home and watched the TV. When Charla came home, I told her that I had applied for a job and hoped to hear from the manager in about a week. She was happy but warned me not to be too hopeful as lots of folks were looking for work. She said I needed to apply for lots of jobs and handed me the Sunday *New York Times* help wanted section to read. With a red marker, I circled the jobs that were for trainees. Charla encouraged me to apply with the company that she works for, MetLife. So, Tuesday I went to work with her and met with the Human Resources manager, Miss Loews. After filling out the employment application, she gave me an interview right away. Then I went to apply with other positions. I continued going out every day, but I really had my heart set on working for Starbucks.

"On Monday, I received a call from Mr. Cornell. He told me that after conferring with his supervisor they decided to hire me. I was beyond thrilled. I was told to report to the training center on Tuesday at 9 a.m. at Fifth Avenue. I met all the other hopefuls, and we received the training manual. We were to study it at home. The first thing they did was to give us coffee to drink. You know how I hate the taste of coffee, but I didn't have a choice. We swilled around samples of Dunkin' Donuts coffee and Au Bon Pain and other brands I can't recall right now. They all tasted nasty. But I stuck with it because I ain't no quitter. After two weeks, we were ready to begin working in the store. I got my first choice, the twenty-four-hour Astor Place location.

"I observed the experienced baristas make the drinks. There were so many to remember, but I had studied the manual faithfully. I was allowed to make a few drinks under their watchful eyes. I managed to screw up some of the drinks, but my supervisor just redid them, and they did holler at me for messing up. I also used the cash register. Little by little, I absorbed the process and became really adept at making drinks. They allowed us each one free drink per hour. At first, I only drank the non-coffee drinks, but the aroma of coffee wafting through the air beckoned to me, and I decided to try the coffee-based drinks. Slowly I sipped them, savoring the smooth, mellow flavor, no longer wanting to spit them out. Coffee seduced me, and it was at that point that I became an addict. Anytime I made someone's drink, I surreptitiously took a sip. This went on for about eight months until I was caught by a customer. I was reprimanded by my manager and given a demerit. I tried to stop, but it was beyond my control. I was caught twice more and finally fired. I confided in Charla about my addiction, but she wasn't sympathetic to my predicament. She kicked me out of the apartment and got another roommate.

"I was so bereft and upset that I wandered the streets of New York. I got an empty, plastic Starbucks cup and begged the commuters for change for coffee. I had a man approach me with an offer to purchase a cup of coffee for me, but he insisted on buying me the cheap kind, and I informed him that my taste runs to the expensive java, only Starbucks will do. He cursed me, spat on my face, and said that I was just a dirty slug. I slunk away, but my pride was intact. I found a warm spot over a heated grate and parked my butt on it. It was a swanky neighborhood, 5th Avenue and 68th Street. Someone gave me a tattered blanket and a soot-covered pillow. I lived exclusively on coffee, milk, and sugar. I slowly transformed into a street urchin. After a while, I got sick of living in the street and decided to hitchhike home. I met many interesting folks who gave me a lift, and I felt safe with all of them. And that's how I got back here."

Unbeknown to Darla and Bertha, Wally had taken the yellow pages and looked up a rehab center for addicts. He picked Quiet Times since it was located about ten miles away. After Wally made the call, he then joined Bertha and Darla. He overheard Darla mention she was an addict but didn't know it was to coffee. Finally, he took Darla's hand and said, "We need to schedule an intervention for you so you can become free of drugs. I called the rehab center, and they will be showing up in about an hour. I love you too much to let you throw your life away on nonsense."

"Dad, you're mistaken I'm only addicted to coffee. I've never tried any drugs in my life."

Second Chance

It's a strange thing how one incident can change a person's life forever. Even though I grew up in a "father knows best" kind of town, I always was a fearful person. My parents, Ed and June, were overprotective of me and held onto me the way they held onto their youth. This created my anxiety. Even though I was only five years old at the time, I have a vivid memory of my Aunt Emma visiting us. I hid behind my mother's purple cotton skirt because I feared all visitors. I looked like a bandit, with my shy eyes peeking out from behind the billowy fabric.

In school, I always kept to myself. Although I had many opportunities, I chose not to help any of the bullied children. I looked away from their pleading eyes, afraid that my involvement would make me a target of those same bullies. Then on that fateful day, sixteen years later, which is indelibly imprinted on my traumatized brain, I questioned how one human could so hate another person that they could casually contemplate how to end that person's life.

My eyes beheld the branches in their naked state, having shed the abundant coat of fall leaves. Fragmented shards of liquid pierced my ruby cheeks. I yearned to flee the mundane, to unburden and unfetter my heart to a listening ear. As the wind's fingers gently caressed my shoulder-length brown hair, I heard the distinctive sound of a bee's symphony. I freed my uninvited guest by lowering the car window. Eggs, butter, milk, bread. Suddenly, I saw something glint out of the corner of my eye. I glanced at the car to my left. What I saw next was the thing that nightmares are made of. The bizarre-looking driver leaned over, and in his left hand, he had a butcher knife raised over the passenger side. With a maniacal smile dotting his mouth, he plunged the knife in the direction of a young woman's heart. I was mesmerized; my first thought was that this couldn't be happening. They must be filming a movie. Suddenly the light changed, and I heard honks from the car behind me. The driver next to me gunned his motor and sped up. The next thing I knew, I was tailing him. He changed lanes various times, and I followed his lead. He must have known that I was there. I started fumbling in my purse for my cell phone. After a few minutes, he suddenly slowed down, pushed the body out of his car, and sped up and drove away. Although I was fully conscious of the risk, I slowed to a stop and jumped out. Then I quickly dialed 911.

"What's your emergency, please?"

"I just witnessed an attempted murder. A man just stabbed a woman in her chest, and she is bleeding profusely. The red fluid is covering everything, including my hands. Help me.

"Please hurry. She can't hold on much longer."

"Okay, miss. What is your name?"

"My name is Allegra Collazo. Please send someone now. I think she is dying."

"Allegra, I have the police on the other line. I need to know where exactly you are."

"I'm on the shoulder of I-95 near exit ten. There is a large sign advertising Motel 6. I see another sign with a McDonald's logo."

"Okay, I've given the officers your location. They should be there in a few minutes. I need you to keep talking to me. Is the woman still breathing?"

"Yes, but it sounds very faint. I've tried to find her pulse, but her arms are too slippery. I'll try talking to her." I said in a soft voice, "Miss, are you okay?" I turned my attention back to the dispatcher. "She's groaning. Is there anything I can do to stop the bleeding?

"Please hang on. Don't die on me."

"Do you have some rags? If not, you can tear some strips from a shirt and apply pressure. If you don't know how to do this, I can talk you though it."

"Wait, I hear the police sirens." A burly police officer and his emaciated-looking partner emerged from the cop car. "Oh, thank God you're here. Please help her."

"Okay, miss, we'll take it from here. Let me speak to the dispatcher."

I was in shock, and the next thing I knew, I fainted. Strong arms put me in the police cruiser as we waited for the arrival of the ambulance. The sirens roused me from my sleep. I looked around, and at first, I thought I was safe in my bed. But I soon remembered the horror of the last few hours and started screaming. Officer Gallagher rushed over and tried to comfort me. His soft-spoken words were a relief to my shaken body. I began to relax, and then they drove me to Lakeview Hospital. The two officers interviewed me as a doctor examined the victim. She was rushed into surgery.

"Miss Collazo, we need to interview you about this heinous crime. We'll make it as brief as possible. Again, I want to thank you for getting involved and helping our Jane Doe. Detective Bo Richards will be questioning you. Excuse me, Doc, but can we use the conference room for about fifteen minutes? Great, thanks. Allegra, please follow me."

As we walked down the long corridor, I felt like I was signing my death certificate. I somehow knew that this fiend would find me and leave no living witnesses. After they ushered me into the room, we sat on dotted pink vinyl chairs clustered around an oblong oak table.

"Miss Collazo, do you mind if I record this session? Everything we say will be transcribed."

"No, that's fine. Please, call me Allegra. I just want to preface this by saying that this is so unlike me. I always mind my own business. It's safer that way."

"Well, in my profession, I've met many people from various backgrounds. It's interesting how when we are faced with stressful situations, we run on pure adrenaline. There usually is no time to think. When did this incident take place?"

"I think it was about 10 a.m. I was mentally noting what items I needed to pick up from Ralph's Supermarket."

"Then what transpired?"

"For some reason, I glanced at the car to my left. Then I observed the vicious slicing of flesh."

"Can you describe the perpetrator?"

"Yes, I think he wore a grotesque Halloween mask. It resembled Batman's nemesis, The Joker. I saw his hair; it was kind of disheveled, black peppered with white. His eyes were almost black. He had a crazy grin."

I felt so utterly helpless. It gnawed on my nerves and put me in a state of dread.

"Allegra, are you sure it was a man? Since this person was masked, could it have been a woman?"

"Actually, I'm not sure. Right now, I'm so confused. I was focused more on the plunging of the blade."

"Did you perchance get a good look at the color and make or model of the vehicle?"

"Yes. It was a dark blue car, a Mazda 360zx. There were patches of rust on the body. I was able to get a partial license plate number since he kept weaving in and out of traffic. I jotted it down. Here's the slip of paper."

"Okay, thank you, Allegra, for your cooperation."

This felt more like an interrogation than an interview.

Then the officers drove me home. After entering my abode, I immediately locked all the doors. Then I drew a hot bath. I scrubbed until raw trying to erase all traces of the blood stains. I soaked in the tub for about an hour, then toweled dry and put on a red terry cloth bathrobe. Then I plopped down in front of the television and turned on the news.

"The top story of the day is the attempted murder of a 'Jane Doe.' Police are scouring the neighborhood looking for the culprit responsible for the horrendous crime. If you have any information, please contact Crime Stoppers at (800) 596-TIPS."

Then I dialed the tow truck company.

"Hello, Jeremy, this is Allegra. I know it's late, but I need my car towed from I-95 near exit ten. I left the keys on the front seat. Tell Jim I'll send him a check. You can leave the car in front of my garage. Thanks."

I set my alarm clock for 9 a.m. At 6 a.m., I suddenly awoke with a start to the jangling of the phone.

I was awoken to a muffled male voice that said, "Allegra, this is a friendly warning; you better not say anything to the cops; otherwise, you'll join that bitch at the hospital."

"Who is this? Why are you threatening me?"

Then the line went dead. I immediately dialed the police.

"Hello, is Detective Richards there? Please tell him to call Allegra Collazo at (609) 724-3900. Tell him it's an emergency."

I threw on some clothes and then grabbed a quick breakfast of oatmeal and some java. After waiting a couple of hours for Detective Richards to return my call, I made up my mind to take a drive. As I drove around aimlessly, I decided to visit the wounded woman because I was concerned about her welfare. When I arrived, there was a police cruiser out front. I was met by the officers and ushered into an empty room.

"Allegra, we ran the partial license plate you gave us through the computer. It turns out that the vehicle is registered to a Mr. Jim Monroe."

"No, it can't be. He's the owner of the Tic Tac Tow Truck Company. Are you sure?"

"There's no doubt about it. Since the victim refused to give us her identity and name her attacker, the FBI was called in."

"Detective Richards, I received a threatening phone call this morning. It sounded like the voice was disguised. I'm really scared."

"Allegra, since you are a witness to this gruesome event, Lieutenant Craig would like to ask you a question."

"Miss Collazo, you do have the option of joining the Witness Protection Program. This encompasses the changing of your identity. You will be relocated under a police escort. If you need time to think it over, that's fine. Do you have any family that you could discuss this with?"

"No, I'm alone now. My parents passed away about three months ago, and I think my aunt died about five years ago. Although I'll miss the small-town atmosphere of Silverton, I'm now ready for a change."

"Okay, Captain Gallagher will take you home so you can pack. I hope everything works out well for you."

My tears flowed freely as we approached my house. I began the arduous process of packing my possessions. It took hours. I stayed up all night. I left Silverton for the first time in my twenty-six years at 3 p.m. I'm looking forward to my new life.

Murder Most Fowl

The deed is done. Sally murdered her husband Frank after he criticized her cooking one too many times. She bludgeoned him to death with a drumstick. Sally dragged Frank's body into the bathroom and threw it into the bathtub. Who would have thought that a woman like her (barely 5' and ninety-five pounds) could have felled a giant of a man (all 6'4" with two hundred pounds of muscle)? After severing his jugular vein, she poured out all the spurting blood from his body and then proceeded to wash it down the drain. Afterward, she painstakingly chopped him into little pieces with a sharp knife. Her expertise in deboning a chicken served her well. She went into the kitchen, and she grabbed two large plastic see-through garbage bags from a box. She put a pair of yellow rubber gloves on her hands, and after opening the bags, she gingerly placed all of the squishy pieces inside. She then sealed the bag with a plastic twist tie. After removing her gloves, she ran to her clothes closet and pulled a suitcase covered with travel stickers from the shelf. Sally tossed the suitcase on the bed. She flung it open and put the bags inside and shut the suitcase.

As she packed, she thought about all the things that led her to this unplanned murder. Although the marriage lasted for thirty long years, it was peppered with violent outbursts. Throughout this time, she tolerated the verbal abuse heaped upon her by dear husband Frank and stood by him despite his womanizing. The world saw the smile she pasted on her face every day for years. She had supported him when he decided to disinherit their three adult children—Suzy, thirty; Kate, twenty-six; and Arnie, twenty-two—for no reason other than their estrangement from him. Because of his nasty disposition, he managed to alienate all the family members as well as any remaining friends. She became his virtual slave. He once told her that the only reason he married her was because she could cook, clean, and warm his bed. He lavished more attention on Zoe the cat than she received in all the years she was married to this jerk. She vividly remembers his boss, Joe, who so despised him that when Frank retired, instead of receiving the coveted gold watch, his gift was a poisonous asp. After Frank opened the box and realized what it contained, he quickly covered it. The police were called, and she remembered the newspaper photo of Joe handcuffed but still defiant. He managed to spit in Frank's face before being hauled off to jail.

Sally then directed her attention to the task of cleaning up the gory mess.

She used a whole bottle of bleach. With her scrub brush, she banished all signs of blood. In a panic, Sally wondered where she would dispose of the evidence. Then she remembered the bus station. She unlocked her door and dragged the suitcase down the steps. With each thump, sweat started to pour down her face. Her nosy landlady Minerva lived downstairs, and Sally was afraid she would hear the noise. After exiting her building, Sally hailed a cab, hoping that the driver couldn't sense the smell of death. Had any of the body fluids seeped through the suitcase? In a calm, controlled voice she told the driver, "Mac," "Take me to the Port Authority Bus Terminal." After they arrived there, she handed the driver a fifty-dollar bill and told him to keep the large remainder as his tip.

Mac dutifully removed the suitcase from the trunk of the cab. He then remarked to her, "This suitcase weighs a ton, it feels like a body is in here." Sally laughed nervously and took the suitcase from the cabdriver. After profusely thanking him, she dragged the suitcase to the locker. Sally deposited the coins into the slot and pulled the door open. She chose locker number thirty-three as that's the one they always used when they traveled. She pushed the suitcase into the locker and watched as the door slammed shut. She removed the key and pocketed it.

As Sally waited for a cab back, she formulated her story. Since Frank was the consummate womanizer, she would just tell anyone who inquired as to his whereabouts that he ran away with his girlfriend. Of course, she will first have to forge a good-bye letter in his handwriting. Also, she will have to dispose of all his belongings. Perhaps Jeff from the dump will help her? After all, he has always had a soft spot in his heart for her.

Morning Tradition

The bathroom of our family's apartment became a focal point of my life as a child. For here is where I bonded with my dad, Courtland. I fondly remember the routine we built up every day. It would be early morning when my father switched the lights on, bathing the room in a soft halo glow. This had the effect of highlighting the garish walls with their peeling yellow paint. I watched my father shaving from my perch standing on the toilet seat, looking over the cold, hard floor covered with small tan tiles. He would reach for a razor blade and snap it into the head of the shaver. After laying it down on the ledge of the sink, he would then turn on the faucet and cup his hands. After he put the glistening water on his face, he would reach for the red can of Barbasol shaving cream. He pushed down on the nozzle, and out shot a creamy stream of foam. He rubbed the cream between his big, warm hands to soften it. A slight scent of mint would tickle my nose. He would then apply it to his face in a circular motion. After rinsing his hands and reaching for the shaver, he would begin the process of shaving his whiskers. His left hand would push the skin up while his right hand would move the blade rhythmically down his face. As the water flowed from the faucet, he ran the slicing blade through this gushing waterfall. I don't remember us talking; I was mesmerized by all that I observed. On he plowed—shaving, rinsing, shaving, rinsing, shaving, rinsing, until he completed his focused task. Then on to the other side of his face he went. His left hand gripped the shaver while his right hand pushed up on the skin. So much repetition, yet so fascinating to a three-year-old child. When the task was complete, he would reach for the clean hand towel draped on the towel rack. His fingertips impatiently pulled it, and with much gusto, he patted his face dry.

My reward always came after his routine. He picked me up by the waist and swung me around in a circle. He laughed while I gleefully absorbed his loving attention. Snuggled in the cocoon of his arms, I felt just like a princess, safe and warm in my castle.

"The Coin Collection"

My sister gave me a pile of coins; some were bright and shiny, while others were older and dull. My father, Courtland, the quintessential coin collector, accumulated foreign currency from his travels abroad. Some of the places he visited were Switzerland, Canada, Japan, England, and a host of other countries too numerous to list. When he died, his collection was divided equally among the four children. This was our inheritance.

His death was a drawn-out process. He was basically "murdered" by his second wife, Judith. His lungs filled with her secondhand smoke over the thirty odd years they were together, and this directly caused his premature death at seventy-five. The death certificate stated: "Contributing factor, smoking." He was a non-smoker, and his wife was a chain smoker. The date of his death is indelibly seared in my brain, October 21, 2002. The coins represented to me a wasted life. He was never able to spend them due to his untimely death.

I didn't feel any sentimental value for the coins, so I decided to sell them. I went to a store named Domenico that buys and sells stamps and coins. I learned they had no value due to the fact that each country's currency had changed, such as the Franc had become the Euro. I then decided to place an advertisement to sell them at ten cents each in a free newspaper called *LOOT*. A Russian woman called, and I told her that the coins were still available for sale. She arrived at my home on a Friday afternoon. After we exchanged pleasantries, we got down to business. Her name was Livia. She explained to me that she was purchasing these coins for her nephew in Russia who collects foreign coins. I laid out the coins on the dining room table. Livia picked the coins that interested her. After choosing two hundred coins, she placed a twenty-dollar bill in my hand. I was elated since this was pure profit for me.

I now keep the coins as a painful reminder of my father's untimely death in full view on my night table. There are many possibilities for these coins. It is possible to create a vest from them using pliable wire twisting around each coin and connecting them together. It would be functional attire or wearable art. A time capsule with other memorabilia from the year 2002 is another possibility. I could also create a dollhouse by using the coins to glue them to the roof. From my point of view, I don't regard the coins in the same way my father did.

Fear Feeds the Famine of Finality

"The greatness of a nation and its moral progress can be judged by the way its animals are treated." The aforementioned quote by Mohandas K. Gandhi shows the relationship between our treatment of the animals in our care and the resulting prosperity and advancement of a country.

Let us suppose that Gandhi had a younger sister, named Sunita, who lived at home under the domineering rule of her father, Aziz. While Gandhi was gallivanting, expounding his political aspirations and trying to save the world, Sunita was witnessing Aziz's mistreatment of her mother, Priya.

Frustrated by her lack of freedom and the constant threats of her drunken father's rantings, Sunita resorted to torturing her defenseless kitten, Somalia. Although Somalia used her sharp claws to defend herself, she was no match for Sunita's escalating rage. One day, Sunita decided to hang Somalia on metal meat hooks by her ears. After letting her hang for about three hours, she decided to put the cat out of her misery by cutting her open with a cleaver and eviscerating her. This did nothing to dampen her burgeoning frustration, so Sunita grabbed a whip, raced out to their barn, and proceeded to beat the family's horse, Chapati. She did this until he was raw and bleeding, thus drenching Sunita's sari in crimson gore. Chapati's whinnying brought the stable hand running. After ascertaining who inflicted the almost fatal beating, he raised the alarm. Aziz was summoned, and after hearing the story, his wrath aroused; he grabbed Sunita's wrist and dragged her into the house. Aziz threw her in her room and slammed the door so hard that it splintered. Then he fished out the key from his shirt pocket and secured the lock. After finding out about Chapati's condition, he threatened to whip Sunita senseless. He then summoned the vet.

Twenty-five-year-old Gandhi received an urgent phone call from his father regarding his sister Sunita, as he was leading the non-violent demonstrators down the streets of Calcutta trying to abolish the caste system. Aziz stressed that Sunita's behavior was out of control, and they needed Gandhi's calming influence to settle her down. Gandhi immediately jumped into his Rolls Royce and had his chauffeur drive him to his father's house.

Sunita decided to escape the inevitable beating her father was determined to inflict upon her. Hidden away underneath her bed lay a bamboo-woven suitcase packed full of pastel saris waiting for this very moment. Being a voracious reader, she remembered a line from her favorite book, *The Great*

Escape, in which the heroine uttered, "I took the bobby pin from my long flowing hair and quietly inserted it into the lock. I gently fiddled with it until the lock opened and my escape was imminent." Sunita followed the plan to a tee. Her slippered footsteps padded down the stairs. When she reached the bottom of the stairs, she looked both ways, listening for any sounds. The only sound she heard was the ticking of the clock. She eased the heavy wooden door open and sprinted toward the forest. Freedom was within reach of her grasp, and she was determined to become a non-entity to her family. As she fled, she heard her father's bellowing voice calling her name. After about an hour of running, she slowed her pace. Because the heavy suitcase was impeding her progress, she decided to hide it behind one of the evergreen trees, planning on returning later to retrieve it. The forest echoed her heartbeat. Silence ensued. Her feet felt cold, and when she looked down, she noticed her slippers were in tatters. She hesitantly approached the house of her Aunt Indira. With raised fists, she began furiously beating on the door, her breathing in gasps.

After Indira took in Sunita's disheveled appearance, she calmly allowed her to enter her house. Sunita was sure her aunt would side with her since, forty years previously, Aziz had tried to force Indira into an arranged marriage. After hearing Sunita's tale of woe, she told Sunita that she must return home to her parents as that was the only honorable thing to do. Sunita reached for the letter opener and stabbed herself in the heart. Her body was returned to her family in a horse-drawn wagon. The suicide act was so disgraceful to her family that instead of burying her, her body was set afire on the funeral pyre in Porbandar, India.

Trading Places

This morning I woke up at 7:00 a.m. and yawned. I suffer from insomnia, and I never get enough beauty sleep. I leisurely stretched my limbs and then proceeded to find a scratching post. Today I chose Nancy's wooden dresser to sharpen my claws, but I'm not particular where I do this, so most of the furniture is marked by me. I extend my sharp front claws and start from the top drawer and slide my nails down toward the floor.

After this exercise, my thirst needs to be quenched, so I go in search of liquid refreshment. I have three options to satisfy my dry, parched tongue. The tub water is the Perrier of H2O; the sink is my next choice, and I usually turn up my nose at the toilet water. Next, I jump into the tub and start my symphony of meowing and wait for one of my giant subjects to turn on the spigot. Lila always performs this task for me, as I have her wrapped around my little paw. Nancy is another matter altogether. She is very stubborn and insists on filling up my blue plastic bowl with sink water and places it beside my food dish. Afterward, I casually stroll over to my dry, unappetizing meal, sniff its contents, and then gingerly devour a small portion. After all, I do have to watch my figure. Then it's off to the privy where I do my business. I wish Nancy would clean my cat box more often; it sure does stink. I find I have a compulsion to groom myself everyday, although I do worry about spitting up those nasty hairballs.

The rest of the day is for fun. I play with my toys, chase pieces of plastic to chew on, and generally have an enjoyable time. I'm always looking forward to a tasty morsel, so when I spot those brown bugs with hard shells skittle by me, I immediately pounce. I toss them around like hockey pucks until they're dead, and then I pop them into my mouth. I love the crunching sound and am ecstatic when the juices dribble down my chin. I always leave a trail of fur everywhere, and why not? I'm the queen of this castle.

When I tire of all this, I take a nap on the top of the tall, white Ikea dresser. I make sure my paws are tucked underneath my body so I am comfortable enough to fall asleep. Then I'm awakened from my slumber by Nancy, who is clamoring for my attention. I climb up onto her shoulder and give her a big hug. As I'm purring, she squeezes me, and I'm in my bliss. When I've had my fill of love, I jump down onto the floor. Then I'm off to amuse myself further.

If I'm having an especially interesting dream and someone disturbs me, my pupils enlarge, and you better watch out for my ensuing wrath. I'm an expert swordsman where my sharp talons are concerned, and I have been known to leave painful puncture marks on my enemies. Because of my sure footing, I love jumping from one place to another.

My favorite spot in the whole apartment is the window ledge. While my tail is whipping from side to side, I watch the cars, trucks, and giants go by. The gentle breeze of the wind caresses my furry face and makes me want to jump out of the window and join the action. Ain't life wonderful? I sometimes think about running away as my freedom is but a closed door away. I could pack my tiny suitcase with all my toys and write a letter To Whom It May Concern. But since I have all the comforts of home, why should I risk ending up a homeless feline forced to eat out of garbage cans? No, I think I'll just stay put and enjoy my time with my human companions, although I hope they get the hint and start feeding me canned food because I'm worth it.

Personal Belief

Live Free or Die. To most people these words conjure up the concept of freedom. They were originally uttered by General John Stark in July 1809. They are the official motto of New Hampshire. But, to me, they literally mean live free or die. My mantra is "Why should I pay for anything?" Let me explain. Recently I attended a CUNY job fair. Instead of actually trying to find a job, my focus was on obtaining free items such as pens, pencils, tape measures, etc. The Sunday newspaper contained a coupon for a free bar or bag of chocolate, value up to $2.99. My actual outlay of money was fifty-eight cents, the cost of the item minus the coupon plus tax. I was able to find three of these coupons.

I have taken other peoples discards and transformed them into cold hard cash. My neighbors' garbage has helped this unemployed college student immensely. Two sterling silver candy dishes were sold to Empire Diamond and Gold Buying Service for $35.00. Lost MetroCards of varying amounts have benefited my children and friends. A discarded Starbucks gift card yielded a ten-dollar balance, which I promptly converted to twenty-five dollars by honest means. Because of this unexpected windfall, I treated a friend to a tall blackberry green tea Frappuccino. To my horror, they were out of blackberry syrup. I asked the manager for a replacement coupon, as did my friend. I now had two free, any-size drink coupons plus the balance of my Starbucks gift card. I used the remaining balance on my gift card to purchase a tuna sandwich. I still had those two free, any-size drink coupons burning a hole in my pocket. I used each one to get a venti blackberry green tea Frappuccino.

Many people overlook the windfall banks are now offering to get new customers. Last year I opened a checking account at Valley National Bank. For my initial deposit of a check, I received, via coupon, a free fifty dollars from the bank which was credited to my account. After mentioning to the account representative that I was a college student and loved discounts, she promptly threw in two mugs and a pen. I was positively beaming. I told my friend Susie about this great offer, but unfortunately, she already had an account with this bank. We went there anyway, and her friendly manner got her two mugs, plus she mentioned the offer the bank gave when opening a holiday club account. The account representative wasn't sure if they had any more of the glass cutting boards/trays, but she would check in the back. Lo and behold, she found them, and we each received one.

The best part of getting free stuff is sharing my bounty with others. Although most scavengers live deep in the ocean, I consider myself a land scavenger. As I walk down the street, my eyes are constantly scanning the pavement for pennies etc. Do some curbside shopping today!

Free to Be a Tree

My whole existence is rooted to one spot. I am proud and a majestic oak tree.

Fall is my favorite season of the year. The cool breeze tickles my leaves, and they sway like a wind chime. My color transforms from green to yellow and, finally, to a fiery red. When I can no longer hold them to me, I scatter my dead leaves to the ground where they provide a trampoline for little feet. The children's laughter furnishes a refrain from my troubling thoughts. As I face winter naked and exposed for all the world to see, I am bereft and inconsolable.

During the summer, I provide shade to picnickers as they recline against my trunk eating sticky slices of watermelon. As the smell of barbecuing hamburgers, hot dogs, and veggies wafts toward my nose, the enticing aroma stirs my hunger. Unfortunately, I am never invited to partake from any of this feast. The ensuing army of ants crawling over my bark sends chills down my spine.

The sparrows find refuge on my limbs during an angry thunderstorm. I cradle their nests in my outstretched arms, patiently awaiting their birth. The woodpeckers come in droves to knock on my door, but they receive no reply. They leave behind deep indentations that resemble pock-marked acne.

Through the process of photosynthesis, I greedily inhale the carbon dioxide and slowly exhale precious oxygen that benefits all living creatures.

I observe people hurrying by me, their destinations unsure, while the occasional dog lifts his leg to salute me while watering my soil. I cringe when I see lovers strolling toward me. The male of the species opens the glinting switchblade, which pierces my bark. The pain of this assault travels up and down my body. My nerves recoil in agony. It is a thousand times worse than a paper cut. My scars run deep with the names of amorous couples and outlines of silly hearts.

I hide my age well. My inner rings are the only evidence to my fading glory. When I grow old, I fear the ax man cometh. He wields his weapon skillfully. Soon I will become a pile of kindling to make a blazing fire so someone can warm his or her hands on a chilly winter's night. After the fire completely consumes me, I turn into ash, which is then thrown onto the soil to nourish it, and so the cycle of life continues.

Nation Mourns Lady of the Evening

On January 17, 2007 at 7 p.m., Lucy "Hooker" Hadley passed away at the age of fifty-seven. Miss Hadley died at Methodist Hospital of Necrotizing Fascilitis, also known as the flesh-eating disease. She leaves behind a husband, Gerard, forty-seven; two sons, Basil Hadley, twenty-five, Bo "Bird" Hadley, twenty-two; and one daughter, Summer Hadley, twenty-seven. Miss Hadley became acquainted with her future profession as "an accidental tourist" while vacationing in Florence, Italy, during the summer of 1967. She was approached by a handsome stranger and introduced into the world of prostitution. Thus, began her delightful descent into the abyss of apathy. Photos of her shaking her naked booty can be viewed at www.cheaptrick.com. Miss Hadley was known in California as the Monterey Madam. She won a Lifetime Achievement Award for passing on a slew of sexually transmitted diseases to her unsuspecting Johns. She is also listed in the Guinness Book of World Records for having the most lovers, three thousand, during a period of one year, in 2000. She gave lectures on the history of prostitution at many prestigious universities, including Harvard, Princeton, and Yale. Although her fee was exorbitant, all attendees acknowledged that she was well worth the price. Services will be held at 7 p.m. on January 19, 2007, at Bastardi and Sons Funeral Home, 169 Easy Lay Way, Malibu, CA. In lieu of flowers, monetary donations can be made to the NF Foundation to abolish this awful disease.

The Wake

Lucy's family arrived at 6:30 p.m. Her husband immediately approached the cherrywood table, which prominently displayed photos of Lucy at various stages in her life, beginning from her early childhood to her acceptance of her many awards. Afterward, her family walked toward the closed casket containing her rotting flesh. The mahogany casket was hand carved with beautiful scenes of angels flying toward the heavens. The lining was a soft pastel pink made of the finest silk. The mortician warned her family beforehand that the wounds she had were so extensive that if the general public were to view her face, some people would be sure to faint at the gruesome sight.

As the family lovingly stroked the smooth wood of the coffin, Lucy's friends and neighbors began to trickle in. On a stand to the left of the room stood an opened book with blue-lined, white parchment paper for everyone to sign their names, a keepsake for the grieving family. The stragglers then went to pay their respects to the family and marched by the coffin. Finally, after Pastor Roberts arrived at 7 p.m. sharp, everyone was told to take their seats. The crowd walked over and settled their heinies comfortably into the gold-brocaded, fleur-de-lis-backed emerald green chairs. As Pastor Roberts was delivering the eulogy, Betty May, a good friend of Lucy's, started to speak to June Bug, a casual acquaintance of Lucy's, about Lucy's secret life. "That woman was screwing everyone's husband, and Pastor Roberts is praising her kindness. What kind of hypocrisy is this?"

To which June Bug replied, "How do you know about that? Why, I always thought that was just a nasty rumor. I try never to pay attention to gossip; half the time you can never verify anything." That shut Betty May's mouth real quick.

As Pastor Roberts' talk was rambling and tears were coursing down his cheeks, he suddenly looked up at all the grieving faces and announced that he was the blood father of Summer. Shock registered on everyone's face, and people started murmuring their outrage at the statement issued from Pastor Roberts' mouth. Lucy's husband Gerard jumped up from his chair, overturning it, and, with raised fist, shouted, "How dare you besmirch my loving wife's memory with such smut. Do you have any proof for such a shocking statement?

"As a matter of fact, I do," said Pastor Roberts. "Last month I took a DNA test to prove my paternity. I have suspected for years that I fathered Summer, but Lucy was hesitant about this. Lucy accompanied me to Dr. Leonard's office for the results of this blood test. He handed me a page of the typewritten analysis with the results 99.999 percent positive that I was indeed this child's parent." This information so infuriated Gerard that he ran up to the front of the room, punched Pastor Roberts square in the mouth, and stormed out of the funeral home. With blood pouring out of his mouth and a few loose teeth dangling, Pastor Roberts staggered out of the room and fainted dead away. Mr. Bastardi immediately called 911 and St. Luke's Hospital. As they waited for the EMS to arrive, a pillow was placed underneath Pastor Roberts' head to make him more comfortable. The crowd couldn't contain their curiosity, so Jeremiah, a friend of the family, was appointed to follow the ambulance and get all the juicy details concerning this secret affair.

Whore Ash

Because of the deteriorating condition of Lucy's body, a family meeting was held where it was unanimously agreed to cremate it. On the 21st of January, Lucy's body was cremated, and the ashes were returned to the family in an antique sterling silver urn engraved with her name and date of death in calligraphic writing. As the family sat at the kitchen table, they contemplated how the ashes were to be dispersed. Summer wanted them scattered over the Pacific Ocean, since her mother loved the sea. Both her sons wanted her buried in the earth, to nourish it, as she was a proponent of green burials. Gerard had an urn especially made for Lucy's ashes. It was shaped like a hot air balloon covered in multi-colored enamel. The aqua blue reminded him of his wife's eyes. The balloon had a glass rod that was inserted into the space between it and the weaved bamboo basket. Two AAA batteries were inserted in the bottom of this, and the tiny on-off white switch was located on the side of the basket. With a push of the button, the mini fan would scatter the swirling ashes within the glass tube. This was a tribute to the freedom Lucy once felt when she sailed away in a hot air balloon over her beloved Malibu. The debate continued long into the night.

The next morning, at 7a.m., there was a frantic knock at the door. Summer opened it, and a bruised and bandaged Pastor Roberts casually strolled through their door and back into their lives. Gerard was ready to sock him, but his sons were fast and held his arms behind his back while pleading with him to hear Pastor Roberts' explanation of his crude behavior. After calming down, Gerard sat on the red paisley couch with his ears cocked to hear an apology. What he heard and saw shook the very foundation of his belief in the sanctity of his marriage. Pastor Roberts handed over a copy of the DNA results listing him as the birth father. Gerard was so distraught that he grabbed the ashes, rushed to the toilet, and, without hesitation, flushed them.

"I Did the Right Thing"

Joe: Hey guys, let's go get a couple of beers. After a day like today, we deserve a break.

Pete: Sounds great. Wait, I'll grab my coat.

Joe: Hurry up, they might find another excuse to keep us on duty.

Pete: Okay, I'm ready. I just need to phone Peggy and tell her I'll be late. (They enter an Irish bar.)

Joe: Hey Mac, give us a round.

Bartender: Okay, Joe, but you need to pay up. It's cash or nothin'.

Joe: Pete, I have to tell you what happened to me before I came to work this morning.

Pete: Joe, if it's about your wife, save it. I'm dealing with my own unhappy family situation.

Joe: Pete, for once just shut up and listen. Stop interrupting me. As I was driving to work this morning, I saw a sight for sore eyes. It sounded like an explosion. I saw the red devil. My first thought was *Oh no, not another terrorist attack*.

Pete: So, you're saying you saw a sunrise? Big deal, I see them all the time. Remember, I get up at five every morning.

Joe: So, I jumped out. The air was as hot at Hades, I couldn't breathe. I raced toward the burning building.

Pete: Can you get to the juicy part? I'm supposed to be home by eight. I've got to put the rug rats to sleep. Story time and all that.

Joe: I heard screams of "help me" coming from inside. I could hear wood crackling and smell burning flesh.

Bartender: Do you wanna another beer?

Pete: Sure do. It looks like we'll be here at least another hour.

Joe: I grabbed the doorknob, but as soon as my fingers touched it, I pulled my hand back because it was hot. The odor of burning flesh stung my nostrils.

(Overhearing)

Bartender: That reminds me of the time when I hosted a barbeque and some jerk poured too much lighter fluid on the charcoal. I ended up burning my hand as a result.

Joe: Shut up! I'm telling a story here. With adrenaline pumping, I kicked open the door, dropped to the floor, and started searching with my fingertips. I touched an unconscious body. I heard a woman moaning. I grabbed her pants and dragged her outside.

(To the bartender)

Pete: I'm sure you found out who the culprit was. I would have made him pay my medical bill.

Joe: The cold air shocked us. I shook the woman and asked her how many other people were still in the house. She screamed, "Get my baby."

Pete: I hate when a kid is found in a burning building. They're so helpless and seem to panic worse than adults. I also can't stand when pets are lost in the confusion of a fire.

Joe: I looked back toward the house, and it was fully engulfed. I flipped open my cell phone and called the fire department. The dispatcher immediately recognized my voice. I gave her the location of the fire and hung up. I felt awful because I knew by the time help arrived, her baby would have perished.

Pete: Joe, you did everything you could have to save those people. Sometimes we can rescue people, and other times, we can't. The fire is stronger than the water we heap upon it. It consumes everything in its path. It becomes the funeral pyre of the dead.

PART 2

Dr. Lichtenstein, a fifty-five-year-old woman, is a stern psychiatrist with a thick German accent. She dispenses advice the way she prescribes pills, very carefully. Teddy Thompson, a popular, well-liked security guard, who is as comfortable around patients as he is around the staff, has an always-smiling face that puts everyone at ease. Milagros Sanchez, a short spitfire in the female form, is as protective of her son, Avitar, as a mother bear. Sharon Mata is curious and quirky. She always gets her interviews.

EXTERNAL: Kings County Hospital

Sharon

Hello everyone. This is Sharon Mata from East Coast News reporting live from Kings County Hospital rehab center. Last week we explored the symptoms of the Avitar Syndrome in-depth. We will now speak to his psychiatrist to find out if this social disease is curable.

Dr. Lichtenstein

Mr. Cologne, tell me more about yourself?

Avitar

Well, Doc, I'm the greatest thing since sliced bread. I'm a reality within myself. You know the saying "No man is an island"; well, I'm complete within myself. I don't need a woman to make me feel like a man.

Dr. Lichtenstein

After observing your behavior and listening to you this past week, I've come to the conclusion that you have a narcissistic personality. In all my years of practice, I've never met anyone like you. Tell me, what is your relationship with your mother.

Avitar

(He pauses and thinks pensively and scratches the side of his head.) Since I'm the first born, my mommy always hugged and kissed me. Anything I wanted, she always got me. Even though we were poor, she bought me a bike and lots of toys. I used to fall asleep on her pillow-soft breasts. She called me her little man. (Avitar starts sucking his thumb.)

Dr. Lichtenstein
Did you ever feel smothered by all this attention she showered upon you? Did she pay attention to your other siblings?

Avitar
I only have one brother. He was always fighting for my mommy's attention. When he broke his leg, I secretly believed he did it on purpose to get Mommy's gentle hugs. That bastard stole my glory. We hate each other (he shows an evil grin).

Dr. Lichtenstein
Mr. Cologne, your outburst is a way to heal your inner child. You must continue to vent your feelings, and then you will get better. Does this make any sense to you?

Avitar
All this psychobabble is making me hungry. Can you get me a roast beef sandwich with lettuce, tomato, and mayo on rye bread with a sour pickle and a Pepsi? Sorry, I don't have any money right now, but can you just charge it to my room?

Dr. Lichtenstein
Avitar, do you think you're in a fancy hotel and you can just order room service? Man, wake up (she pounds the table with her fist for emphasis), you're in a mental ward for rehab. Don't you recognize that you're sick?

Avitar
Maybe I'm deluded. Doc, can you give me a hug? (Avitar jumps out of his chair and advances toward the doctor, who feels threatened.)

Dr. Lichtenstein
Guard, get in here immediately! Restrain this patient and take him back to his room. (She yells out the door.)

Teddy

(Flirting with the nurse, after hearing the doctor's pleas, rushes over and takes Avitar and gently guides him out of the office.) Yo, man, what did you do to the doc? I ain't never seen her so nervous in my life.

Avitar

I just wanted a hug. I miss my mommy so much. (He takes out a bottle of scent and begins to douse himself.)

Teddy

(Coughs.) What is that stuff? (Chokes.) It smells like the bootleg bodega brand of hooker perfume. Give me that. (He grabs it out of Avitar's hand and tosses it into the nearest wastebasket.) That smells like poison, and I don't mean the perfume.

Avitar

But I like the way it smells. My mommy got it for me for my birthday. I'm gonna tell on you, and you're gonna get in big trouble. (He says it in a whiny tone.)

Teddy

Yeah, you do that, little boy. Come on, let's go back to your room.

Avitar

Okay. I got to admire myself in the mirror. (After entering the room, he looks at himself in the full-length mirror and we hear "Mirror, mirror on the wall, who is the handsomest one of all?")

Sharon

(Sharon enters the ward. We hear the clicking sound of her high heels.) Hi, Dr. Lichtenstein. I'm here to do a follow up on the story last week about the Avitar Syndrome. Can we discuss his progress?

Dr. Lichtenstein

I'm sorry, Miss Mata, but that information is confidential. The only way I can give you a progress report is if Mr. Cologne signs a release form. Otherwise, my hands are tied.

Sharon

Well, Doc, I heard that you're a fan of East Coast News. I would be happy to give you a tour of the studio.

Dr. Lichtenstein

Please lower your voice. I don't want my superiors to know about this. Very well, I guess I could dish some dirt on this nutty noodle.

Sharon

Have you made a diagnosis yet? Can he be cured? Is this a very contagious social disorder?

Dr. Lichtenstein

Actually, yes. He has a form of self-love that is excessive and is known as narcissism. The cure rate for this stands at zero. Do you know that his phone number is 1-800-ILOVEME? It's sick. All the men on the East Coast are infected with this virus. There have been a few reported cases of women coming down with it. In Las Vegas, the men have a love affair with the slot machines.

Sharon

Thank you, Doctor, for helping me to understand this disease better. I will inform my television viewers ASAP. (Turns to camera.) Hello everyone. This is Sharon Mata with East Coast News. According to Dr. Lichtenstein, Avitar has a form of self-love called narcissism. Unfortunately, there is no cure. Stay tuned for the next episode of Avitar Cologne's mom rescuing him.

CPSIA information can be obtained
at www.ICGtesting.com
Printed in the USA
BVHW040218160821
614494BV00013B/941